LINCOLN C

200 YEARS— AND STILL COUNTING!

WESLEY R. WILLIS
FOREWORD BY CLAYTON E. RAYMOND

VICTOR BOOKS

a division of SP Publications, Inc.
WHEATON. ILLINOIS 60187

Offices also in Fullerton. California • Whitby. Ontario. Canada • Amersham-on-the-Hill. Bucks. England

Second printing, 1980

Scripture versions used in this book are the *New American Standard Bible* (NASB), © 1960, 1962, 1968, 1972, 1973 by The Lockman Foundation, La Habra, California; and the King James Version (KJV). Used by permission.

Recommended Dewey Decimal Classification: 270.8
   Suggested Subject Headings: SUNDAY SCHOOLS; CHURCH WORK;
   CHRISTIAN EDUCATION.
Library of Congress Catalog Card Number: 79-92009
ISBN: 0-88207-604-3

© 1979 by SP Publications, Inc. All rights reserved
Printed in the United States of America

VICTOR BOOKS
A division of SP Publications, Inc.
P.O. Box 1825 ● Wheaton, Illinois 60187

CONTENTS

Bookstore

3.07

24-0063

66224

FOREWORD

The 200th birthday of the Sunday School movement reminds us of how God has worked in the church. This very readable, selected history of the Sunday School by Dr. Willis helped me understand the past and look forward to the future.

My experience in Christian education has convinced me of the importance of the local church. Sunday School ought to be a vital tool of the church for biblical education, and also for evangelism. But in Sunday Schools, Christians should go first class. We need good, clear objectives and organization in our Sunday Schools. We need well-trained leaders and teachers who are committed to God's Word and to letting the Holy Spirit use them as they teach. We should be strong and aggressive as we take biblical truth that has changed our lives and share it with men, women, and children who will in turn influence other lives.

This book has reaffirmed my dedication to making the Sunday School work within the local church. There is great potential for the Sunday School in the 1980s and beyond. With confident and committed people, balance in the program, biblical objectives, and curriculum based on the Word of God, the Sunday School can't miss. Here's to 300!

CLATE E. RAYMOND
EXECUTIVE DIRECTOR OF THE
INTERNATIONAL CHRISTIAN
EDUCATION ASSOCIATION

1
A Society
in Distress

As you begin reading this, picture yourself living in Gloucester, England in 1780. It is Sunday morning and you are standing in your doorway looking out at the city.

The city! With its people, fun, and excitement. Work in the mills, and money to be made!

No one said it was going to be like this—crowded slums with shabby houses lining narrow, garbage-strewn alleys. You expected so much and receive so little. Why, the walk to draw water here is longer than it was to the well on the farm. And the water on the farm was good. People drink this water and die, but no one seems to care about them.

And the homes! Too many people live in too few homes, that aren't really homes at all. Love grows in homes and people enjoy each other. These are just houses, crowded with people. But it's not just the people. Chickens, geese, and pigs have come to the city, and they live in the houses too. These houses are often dirtier than the pig sties and the chicken coops on the farms, but the animals are needed to supplement your miserable diet in the city.

Even so, few people ever leave the city. Most of them can't read or write, and with no vision of a better future, they grovel in the slime of a subhuman existence. Their lives are little better than those of the animals that share their beds and encroach upon their humanity.

As you stand in your doorway, something seems wrong. This should be just like any one of 100 other Sunday mornings, but it isn't. Somehow today is different. Oh, you still feel tired, but morning always brings a weariness that aches in your joints and bones and muscles. And there is the weariness of the soul that never goes away. A weariness so deep and so constant that you've come to accept it as normal.

And you're not alone. Your friends also experience this same cirrhosis of the will that destroys by attacking their very humanity. It's not just 15-hour days in filthy factories with cruel supervisors. The weariness and exhaustion are products of a life with no meaning, no direction, no reason to continue. When each new morning comes, you confront the most difficult decision of that day—the decision to drag yourself from the filthy straw pallet that you call a bed and face another day without meaning. By night you are too exhausted to eat, too tired to sleep, and too tired to care.

Of course, Sunday is different. It's a day of rest. But still it's not a day of purpose. You can't stop hating your life in one day. In order to endure even that one day, you blot out the other six. Long before nightfall, alcohol has so numbed your senses that most of Sunday is a parenthesis in your life. It ends in a drunken stupor which only adds to the aches and exhaustion, as you greet the rising sun on Monday morning.

Your feeling persists that today something is wrong. The weariness is still there. The city is the same as ever, and it smells just as bad. But something is different. As you stand there, you struggle to think back. It wasn't always this way. When did it all begin?

Back on the farm there was exhaustion, but when you accomplished something, it felt good to be tired. Morning always came too early, but at least there was satisfaction in seeing things grow. And there was the harvest to anticipate. Not always a bumper crop, but usually enough.

But now as you watch the sun rise, the common feelings of hatred and bitterness rise in you too. Why do some have so much and others have so little? Why do your children have to face such a bleak future? As you think about them, despair engulfs you. It sweeps in like a foul, evil-smelling cloud that blots out reality and distorts reason. Is nothing in the world pure and clean and good? Is this despair the best that your children can expect?

The children of the city are the real victims, trapped, with no alternative. They can't read and write; this life is all they ever will know. By age eight they face foul working conditions and the evil influence of those already poisoned by despair and cynicism. They work ten hours a day coiling or pointing the wire used to make pins. They are driven like cattle and treated like dogs.

But the children have to work, because all the income of the entire family barely pays for the absolute necessities. And often it's not enough. Many of your friends and neighbors are in prison because they can't pay their debts. They may be better off there, but how can they pay their debts in prison?

Of course, there is the government! Maybe the leaders know of the problems, but few really understand because they don't like to come to the slums. They do pass more laws and hire more policemen, but stricter law enforcement doesn't solve the real problem. It's like bandaging a gangrenous sore. Even though it may not be seen, it's still there, growing and festering, poisoning the entire system.

The children growing up in this system do anything to survive. They steal and they fight. They destroy whatever they can, taking anything not tied down or locked up. The children are caught in the same vicious trap that ensnares their parents. Crime, vice, immorality. It's a way of life and all they know. The children! Pity the children.

That's it! That's what is different today—the children! As you step into the street, you don't hear the children. They always are fighting, screaming, arguing, and breaking things on Sunday morning. After working all week long, when Sunday comes, they go wild. They rush through the streets like a flood, stealing, breaking, and destroying anything in their paths.

But today it's different. The fighting and screaming are missing. The merchants and vendors have stopped cursing the children and calling the police. Where can the children be? What has happened to them? What is going on? Could it be the school that was started for the children? Have they all been carted off to Sunday School? Is that why it's so quiet?

★ ★ ★ ★ ★ ★ ★ ★ ★ ★ ★ ★ ★

Industrial Revolution

If you had been a member of the lower classes, living in Gloucester, England in the late 1700s, such experiences and circumstances would have been a normal part of life. As the Industrial Revolution gained momentum, children were forced to work long hours in the newly developed factories. Without opportunities for education and moral training, they had only the prospects of hard work, little joy, disease, prison, and death confronting them.

It was in this social context that the modern Sunday School movement was born—a movement that would revolutionize England and sweep around the world. It was to have profound impact on the development of the United States.

The Industrial Revolution that promoted the growth of the cities, and transformed a land of farms into a technological society, generated problems that its people could not solve. Receiving little adult supervision, children grew up with only other children to guide them. Or worse still, they were guided by those who wished to profit from them—the evil, the degenerate, the exploiters.

John Wesley described England during this period: "There is not, on the face of the earth, another nation (at least, that we have heard of) so perfectly dissipated and ungodly; not only so totally 'without God in the world,' but so totally setting Him at defiance. There never was an age, that we read of in history, since Julius Caesar, since Noah, since Adam, wherein dissipation and ungodliness did so generally prevail, both among high and low, rich and poor" (H. Clay Trumbull, *Yale Lectures on the Sunday School,* John D. Wattles, 1888, p. 116).

Irrelevant Religion

Unfortunately, the church did little to counteract the evil influences so prevalent in that society. Indeed, religion had become something aloof and set apart. It was cold, unemotional, and neglectful of many basic spiritual concepts. Ritual, formality, insensitivity, and irrelevance characterized the institutional church, which focused on the upper classes, and which was almost wholly theoretical in nature.

There was a darkness in the land that could only be dispelled by the light of the Gospel. And yet the church—the very institution that should have been spreading the light—rarely addressed the real problems. Bishop J.C. Ryle wrote: "There was darkness in high places, and darkness in low places; darkness in the country, and darkness in town; darkness among rich and darkness among poor—a gross, thick, religious and moral darkness; a darkness that might be felt" *(The Christian Leaders of the Past Century,* London, 1878, p. 13).

Illuminating Rays

It was into this darkness that the light of the Gospel shone. God was pleased to bless the work of two men who started separate works for different reasons. As their ministries grew and developed, the evangelistic ministry of John Wesley and the Sunday School ministry of Robert Raikes combined to provide a powerful beacon to illumine all of England, and from there to shine upon the rest of the world.

Today, two centuries later, we continue to feel the impact of the work started by these two men. In 1780 the first experimental Sunday School, organized by Robert Raikes to meet in Mrs. Meredith's kitchen, was the start of the worldwide movement. No one could have perceived the impact that the organized Sunday School would have upon the world. Individually and corporately we all have benefited from the Sunday School and its results. No nation in the world has been influenced as greatly as the United States.

In the following chapters we'll consider the birth and growth of the Sunday School movement. We'll ask and try to answer questions such as, "Why did the Sunday School movement have much greater long-term impact in the United States than in England?" And, "Why did the Sunday School movement lose momentum in the 20th century?"

We also will consider the various forms of Sunday School that can be found in the United States today. Just as brothers and sisters from the same family sometimes bear only faint resemblance to each other, so there is great diversity among Sunday Schools. Some claim that only one form is valid, while others claim another.

Sunday School seems to have suffered almost as much from those who love it as from those who hate it. Some have called for the total abandonment of Sunday School, while others maintain that it is the lifeblood of the church and of evangelical Christianity. Some have rejected Sunday School completely and totally as "the most wasted hour of the week." Others maintain that, for them, Sunday School has been the single most important experience in the church. We will try to sort out the various perspectives on Sunday School, and probably conclude that there is no "right" Sunday School format for everybody.

Finally, we will examine the biblical purpose of the church and how Sunday School fits into a total church program. Perhaps we have expected too much of a single program; if we ask Sunday School to do everything, it may do nothing well.

The Word of God clearly teaches that the church must provide certain ministries to its members. We will look at Sunday School in light of those biblical mandates and try to evaluate it. We will try to understand what the Sunday School can and cannot do, and how we can organize it most effectively to accomplish its potential in the group life of the church.

As we commemorate the 200th anniversary of the Sunday School movement, we pause in awe. Not that God brought the Sunday School into existence when He did, but that with all of its weaknesses and shortcomings, it has been such a powerful force for good.

Two hundred years—and still counting. Still counting for God and His work in the world. Still counting birthdays because the future remains before us. We will be the ones to write that future and to determine whether or not the Sunday School will continue to grow and influence young and old for God.

2
From Sinai
to Sooty Alley

The idea of Sunday School is far more than 200 years old. The first Sunday School was not organized in England. Just because we can celebrate the 200th birthday of the modern Sunday School movement, does not mean that this is as long as such classes have been in existence. Rather, we can find the forerunner of today's Sunday School in the early history of the Jewish nation.

God intended for the home to be the primary means for instructing children in the Old Testament period. But unfortunately, many parents neglected their responsibility.

One of the main reasons that the nation of Israel turned from God, and eventually was carried into exile, was the failure of the primary agency of instruction—the home. Spiritual disobedience during the time of the Judges was a direct result of parents' failures. As parents neglected their responsibility, they reared a generation of children who rejected God and His Word. "And all that generation also were gathered to their fathers; and there arose another generation after them who did not know the Lord, nor yet the work He had done for Israel. Then the sons of Israel did evil in the sight of the Lord, and they served the Baals" (Jud. 2:10-11).

Synagogue Schools
After its return from captivity, the nation of Israel came to the conclusion that spiritual instruction needed to be reinforced by

groups outside of the home. Soon after the Israelites returned from exile, they organized to help parents in the vital task of spiritual instruction. More than 500 years before Christ, synagogues were established to supplement temple worship. They grew in importance until they became the primary place of worship and instruction. But religious instruction continued as a primary function of the synagogue.

Several hundred years before Christ, a school system was established to instruct each child from the age of five on. As soon as there were ten families in a community, Jewish custom demanded that the leaders establish a school where no teacher would have more than 25 students. When the number of pupils exceeded 25, an assistant was provided. Many school systems today are striving to establish guidelines for a student-teacher ratio that approximate this number of children for each teacher.

Synagogue teachers served without pay, and were highly respected in the community. While these schools certainly should not be called Sunday Schools, they provided the kind of instruction later offered by Sunday Schools.

Early Christian Education

From the time of Christ, education of the Christian community was a vital element in the growth of the church. The Great Commission of Christ to His followers at the end of His earthly ministry was a mandate that included education. The process of making disciples included "teaching them to observe [practice] all that I commanded you . . ." (Matt. 28:19-20). Peter, Paul, and the other disciples strongly emphasized instruction in the Word of God. The first instance of local church organization, recorded in Acts 6, was for the purpose of freeing the disciples to devote their time and energy to teaching the Word.

Soon after the New Testament churches were established, the leaders began schools to instruct new converts and help them grow spiritually. These schools included children and adults of both sexes, with lay men and women teaching. The discussion method of teaching provided full opportunity for questions and answers. The curriculum began with the account of Creation and applied biblical truths to the most practical aspects of the Christian life. These schools were amazingly similar to our Sunday Schools of today, as they emphasized biblical truths, and demonstrated ways in which they applied to life.

Many feel that the phenomenal growth of Christianity in the first four centuries was due primarily to the effective instruction provided by these forerunners of Sunday School. Those opposed to the spread of Christianity feared the impact of such instruction. Julian the Apostate, the emperor of Rome from approximately A.D. 331—363, was determined to take control of the educational system. He felt that if he could keep the children from being influenced by Christian leaders, he could halt the spread of Christianity. He therefore issued an edict that the state would totally control all education, and that no Christians would be allowed to teach in the schools.

In the fourth century after Christ, a man named Gregory, who was in exile from Armenia, was converted to Christianity. When he returned to Armenia, he helped lead the king to accept Christ. Soon, the entire nation officially adopted Christianity. One of the first things that Gregory the Illuminator did was to establish schools similar to Sunday Schools of today, that would help new converts understand and apply Christianity.

The Sixth Council of Constantinople decreed that schools similar to those in city churches should be established in country churches. The purpose of these schools was to instruct pupils in the Bible, which was the primary text used.

The educational emphases fluctuated during the Middle Ages. And so did the vitality of the church and the consistent application of spiritual principles. While the methods and agencies of instruction during these centuries varied greatly, whenever the Bible was taught, Christianity thrived, and when the Bible was not emphasized, there was spiritual darkness and apostasy.

When the spiritual life of the organized church was at its low point, groups that demonstrated biblical Christianity were frequently denounced as heretics. Their endurance under persecution and their purity of life came from their emphasis on Bible instruction. By way of contrast, historians writing about the Inquisition have claimed that the horribly low quality of spiritual life in the organized church came as a direct result of failure to teach the Bible.

Luther's Catechism

In the 1500s during the Protestant Reformation, religious instruction was strongly advocated by the reformers. Luther established schools so that instructors could teach children and youth in a more "simple and interesting manner than from the pulpit." The instructors were to emphasize instruction in the catechism, singing, and prayer. Luther wrote that, "For the Church's sake, Christian schools must be established and maintained." He was convinced that "God maintains the church through the school."

It is unfortunate that we often associate boredom and rote memory with instruction in the catechism. Originally, the catechism was designed as a question/answer starting point for discussion. Luther never expected ritualistic or formal catechetical instruction. He wanted the children to be able to answer the questions, but to go way beyond that. They were supposed to amplify and explain what the various sections meant. The catechism was intended primarily to be a discussion starter.

Philipp Melanchthon, the reformer who worked closely with Luther, suggested setting aside one day a week for religious instruction. These schools were quite similar to Sunday Schools. "After one recitation, the master should explain in a simple and correct manner the Lord's Prayer, the creed, and at another time the Ten Commandments. And he should impress upon the children the essentials, such as fear of God, faith, and good works" (Clyde Manschreck, *Melanchthon: The Quiet Reformer,* Abingdon, 1958, p. 141).

Not only did Melanchthon want children to know the content of the Bible and related curriculum, but he also believed it was absolutely necessary for the teacher to guide the students in applying the principles that had been taught. Melanchthon claimed, "Only through the maintenance of learning can religion and good government endure, and God demands that children be brought up in virtue and piety" *(Ibid.* p. 134).

Jesuit Schools

Indeed many feel that only through the emphasis on schools and religious instruction were the leaders of the Reformation able to create such an impact upon the world. The Roman Catholic Church recognized that the success of the reformers was due to their schools, and they wisely adopted similar methods. As the Jesuits improved upon the instructional system of the reformers, their superior educational system largely halted the progress of the Reformation. Many of the European religious boundaries that were established, as the Jesuits obstructed the progress of the Reformation, remain intact today.

Zinzendorf's Instruction Bands

Schools similar to Sunday Schools were established as few as 50 years before the date we celebrate as the birth of the Sunday School movement. Count Nikolaus von Zinzendorf, leader of the Moravians, founded such schools in the middle 1700s. He was concerned about the growth of his converts, and so organized them into small bands or societies. As these societies met together for study and instruction, Zinzendorf strongly supported instructing children in these groups. His bands were comprised of five to ten converts who would meet regularly to study the Bible and to encourage each other. This pattern also was adopted by John Wesley in his evangelistic campaigns.

Robert Raikes of Gloucester

If religious education schools have been around for thousands of years, why is 1780 considered the beginning of the Sunday School? We celebrate 1780 because this is the year that a gentleman living in Gloucester, England organized a school to instruct the slum children in that city.

Many of us would feel that Robert Raikes' motivation for starting such a school was vastly inferior to the motivation of Gregory, Luther, Melanchthon, or Zinzendorf. And yet 1780 is the generally accepted birthdate of the Sunday School.

Raikes' schools did not grow out of a religious revival, although their beginnings coincided with one. He was not a religious leader, and he did not recruit those with formal religious training to staff his schools. He was not an educator, but rather a newspaper man. He did not look to those who were skilled in educational techniques or philosophies, and yet he set the model for a worldwide educational organization.

In God's sovereignty the physical and social circumstances, along with the intense commitment of one man, enabled an educational format to succeed. Not just to succeed, but to extend in an incredible way, far beyond the wildest expectations of that man and his contemporaries. The historian C.B. Eavey wrote, "And when it is recognized that inadequately trained teachers often serve under poor physical conditions, inefficient administrative arrangements, and with content not well adapted to the needs of pupils, the marvel is that so much good has been accomplished by the Sunday School. So great has been its contribution to the world that it has been called the 'university of the people' " (History of Christian Education, Moody Press, 1964, p. 215).

Robert Raikes was deeply concerned about the working and living conditions of the lower classes. He saw what they had to put up with and keenly felt the injustice, even though he himself was a well-bred newspaper editor. Perhaps it was because of his chosen vocation, or perhaps he was particularly sensitive to the needs of others. He may have seen religion too much talked about, and too little practiced. Whatever his reasons, he determined to do something about the social circumstances of the day.

Robert Raikes had experienced 25 years of failure prior to his experiment with Sunday School. Originally, he had come to the conclusion that the vice, crime, immorality, and poverty in the slum areas of Gloucester, England were the direct results of ignorance. Someone only needed to help the victims of these circumstances develop basic educational skills, he reasoned. Then they would be able to drag themselves out of the quagmire in which they were drowning.

So he developed a program to reach people in the prisons. He would work with persons accused of crimes ranging from debt to the grossest crimes of vice and passion. He met with ex-convicts as they were released from prison, to help them start a new life. With no fanfare, indeed with almost no encouragement, Raikes labored for nearly 25 years to help transform English society. It finally became apparent to him that he was achieving practically nothing. The adults whom he was trying to help returned to their crime and poverty almost as fast as they were released from prison. Needless to say, Robert Raikes became disillusioned and confused.

Contribution, Not Condemnation

When one of the residents of the slum district complained about the rowdy children living in that neighborhood, Raikes reacted differently from most of his contemporaries. He didn't condemn the parents, although they obviously were part of the problem. He didn't call for stricter laws and harsher punishments. Rather, he sought to make a contribution that would help remedy the problem.

He determined that rather than wasting his time trying to get to the adults, he would focus on the children. He wondered "if something could not be done" to help "the little heathen of the neighborhood" grow up to be respectable men and women. He concluded that "the world marches forward on the feet of little children."

Raikes had hit upon a basic truth that others before him had observed. Hundreds of years before Christ, Socrates, the Greek philosopher and teacher, said that if he could, he would get to the highest place in Athens and ask, "What mean ye, fellow citizens, that ye leave no stone unturned in order to scrape together wealth, and yet take so little care of those to whom ye must one day relinquish all?"

Christ encouraged the little children to come to Him so that He could minister to them. Paul encouraged the Ephesian believers to raise their children "in the nurture and admonition of the Lord" (6:4, KJV). This basic principle of influencing adult society by ministering to children is the principle that finally motivated Robert Raikes.

When Raikes turned from his 25-year mission to the parents, and instead, concentrated upon tomorrow's adults, he tried a new experiment that he described as "botanizing in human nature." He determined to do something to break the vicious cycle of ignorance, poverty, vice, and crime.

It was natural that a man like Raikes who was deeply concerned about meeting people's needs, a man who loved children, a man who sought to be part of the solution rather than part of the problem, should answer his own question of whether or not anything could be done. His reply was "Sunday School." And eventually, all of England

and nations around the world echoed and re-echoed the answer, "Sunday School."

Reading, Writing, Morals, and Manners

The purpose of Sunday School, as Raikes conceived it, was different from the concept today. He did not intend it to be a tool of the local church. He did not even see it primarily as a means to teach children the Word of God. He saw it as a means to reach the dregs of English society, to rescue the unfortunate castoffs of a calloused society. His purpose was to teach children to read, since he felt ignorance was their greatest problem.

In addition to teaching children to read and write, Raikes wanted to teach them morals and manners by teaching the Bible. While Bible instruction was not the sole purpose of his schools, Raikes selected the Bible as the best text that could be used for instruction. Bible instruction provided a basis for the teaching of morals.

The children who sorely needed such instruction were employed in the mills and factories six days a week. They obviously had no time for formal schooling, and received no religious instruction. When Sunday came, they ran wild upon the streets, terrorizing the citizenry. Ellwood Cubberley, the well-known educational historian, wrote, "Sunday being a day of rest and the mills and factories closed, the children ran the streets and spent the day in immorality and vice. In the agricultural districts of England, farmers were forced to take special precautions on Sundays to protect their places and crops from the depredation of juvenile offenders" (The History of Education, Houghton Mifflin, 1948, p. 617).

Sunday was the ideal day for Raikes to conduct his school. He would keep the children from their mischief. He also would help solve the basic problem by teaching reading skills, while giving them instruction about God and the Bible.

Bad Boys and Worse Girls

In 1780 Raikes began his experiment. He avoided the temptation to start with a relatively easy group. He chose the worst slum in

Gloucester, where the boys were bad and the girls were worse. Raikes persuaded Mrs. Meredith to allow the school to be taught in her kitchen. She lived on Sooty Alley, so named because of the many chimney sweeps who lived there. It is reported that some of the boys were marched to Sunday School with logs tied to their legs to keep them from running off. The project was so difficult that Mrs. Meredith gave up in despair and the school was moved to the kitchen of Mrs. King, where May Critchley was the teacher. She fared somewhat better, and this school lasted for about two years.

In the first schools, Raikes gathered about 90 children who were employed in the pin factories of Gloucester, and he paid four women a shilling each (about 25 cents), to teach these children on Sundays. Classes were conducted from 10:00 A.M. to noon, and from 1:00 to 5:00 P.M. each Sunday. In order to attend, the children had to have clean hands and faces, and their hair combed. It is likely that this was the only time all week that all three of those conditions were met. The curriculum in the schools consisted of reading and writing, good morals, and religion. There is no question that the women, who taught children whom Raikes described as "miserable little wretches," earned their shillings.

Bobby Wild Goose and His Ragged Regiment

Perhaps the most amazing thing is that these schools accomplished what Raikes had intended! He discovered that the children were able to learn. They were desperate to learn! He found that it was possible to maintain order, and that the children were anxious to attend and please. Soon, Raikes started one school after another. He was the motivating force behind the organization of the schools, and he always financed them out of his personal resources.

In spite of his success, Raikes did not achieve instant fame. Many rejected the whole idea of the Sunday Schools. Some religious leaders maintained that his efforts were useless and that he was engaged in sacrilegious activity on Sunday. Even his friends mocked him, calling him and his children, "Bobby Wild Goose and His Ragged Regiment." Just as today, for every person with an idea and the will to accomplish it, there are many who will explain why it won't work and dutifully prophesy its failure. Undaunted, Raikes continued with the conviction that the concept of Sunday School was worth pursuing.

Raikes was cautious about publicizing his activities until he had acquired some experience. The first official notice of Sunday School was a brief article in the weekly newspaper that Raikes published. The following article, a single paragraph, was printed in the Gloucester *Journal* on November 3, 1783:

> Farmers and other inhabitants of the town and villages complain that they receive more injury to their property on the Sabbath than all the week besides. This in a great measure, proceeds from the lawless state of the younger class, who are allowed to run wild on that day, free from every restraint. To remedy this evil, persons duly qualified are employed to instruct those that cannot read, and those that may have learned to read are taught the Catechism and conducted to church. In those parishes where this plan has been adopted, we are assured that the behavior of the children is greatly civilized.

From this brief description, people began getting excited about the possibilities. Newspaper after newspaper reprinted the article, and thus the news of Raikes' schools spread through all of England and soon to the rest of the world. As we would expect, the reaction to these schools varied greatly. While a few churchmen praised the Sunday Schools, their responses were more often negative.

Some religious leaders questioned the value of the schools. Others condemned them outright as tools of the devil. The Archbishop of Canterbury even went so far as to call together a group to see what could be done to stop the growth of Sunday Schools. Some maintained that those schools violated the Sabbath Day (as if crime and vice didn't). Some didn't want the poor taught since they were afraid it would stimulate rebellion. Others felt that it would create disunity in the church. There also was a whole group of people who were against Sunday Schools because they didn't want their worldly amusements to be curtailed on Sunday.

In spite of these objections, the growth of Sunday Schools surpassed the most optimistic predictions. The vision and commitment of a single individual with a small core of loyal workers, were used by God to establish a work that was to have great and continuing

impact upon the world for over 200 years. It is for these reasons that
Robert Raikes is recognized as the Father of the Sunday School
movement, and that Christians celebrate 1980 as the 200th birthday
of the Sunday School.

3
The Sunday School Comes Alive

The Sunday School movement grew, and as it grew, it spread across England as a tiny flame might spread through a forest. Once the movement had become established, even opposition contributed to its growth. When a flame is tiny, a puff of wind may extinguish it. However, when that flame has grown to a mighty fire, the stronger the wind, the faster the flame spreads. And all of the winds of opposition spread the flame. Since the effectiveness of Sunday School had been demonstrated, those who spoke against the movement merely served to publicize a cause that already had gained substantial support.

There is little doubt that the Gloucester *Journal,* owned by Raikes and his father, played a significant part in the early publicizing of Raikes' activities. The experiment was reported in a simple, factual manner that probably added to its appeal. Without attempting to glamorize or oversell, Raikes acted as a good reporter and shared what was being attempted. The idea gained support from a wide variety of persons, and was publicized further by those who became excited about its possibilities.

Early in the movement a number of influential persons, among them several noblemen, supported the Sunday School. Even more significantly, Queen Charlotte heard what was taking place. Calling for Raikes, she granted him a private audience to hear him relate personally what was being done. The Queen gave her royal endorsement to Raikes and when a fund-raising drive was later initiated, her name headed the subscription list.

It was not only the nobility, however, who supported the Sunday School. It soon became a very popular service opportunity for those who were philanthropically motivated. Fashionable ladies all over England became involved in teaching Sunday Schools. Their status and wealth helped establish a positive identity for the schools, and thereby attracted others to become involved. It is amazing how the imagination and excitement of persons throughout the nation were captured, and how their energy was channeled into such constructive ministry.

Although most of the institutional church actively opposed or tried to ignore the Sunday School, certain influential persons strongly supported its growth. John Newton, an ex-sea captain and slave-trader-turned-preacher, was one of these. Newton eventually became rector of a church in London and a close friend of Raikes. Newton is best known today for his hymns, which include, "How Sweet the Name of Jesus Sounds." The poet and hymn writer William Cowper and the theologian Thomas Scott also supported Raikes and the Sunday School movement.

Lay Leadership

One of the vital elements in the success of Sunday School was the early and continued emphasis on lay leadership. While the initial experiment included paying the teachers, before long this was discontinued and most teachers served for other reasons. By involving a broad cross section of the population, Sunday School became a people's movement, thus increasing the appeal to further involvement.

Many of those who became leaders were highly successful in their own vocations. The skills and talents that enabled them to succeed in their fields were transferred to the organization and administration of Sunday Schools. These highly motivated and energetic men and women often served in Sunday Schools with a zeal greater than they gave to their vocations. It is little wonder that the movement grew. The leaders were educated, concerned, and willing to use their resources, including their money, to establish and promote the schools.

Right Timing

Another important reason for the success of Sunday School was that, in God's providence, Raikes lived at the right time in history. There was a spiritual vacuum in England. Life in the wildly growing cities was generally godless and inhumane, with terrible physical conditions, exploitation of the lower classes, abuse of children, and other intolerable social inequities. By combining an educational mission with a spiritual mission, the Sunday School provided an important answer to these problems.

The way had been prepared for Raikes by John Wesley and others associated with him. Revivals which had begun in England, through the preachings of Wesley and Whitefield, were continued and reinforced by the Sunday School movement. Very early in the history of the Sunday School, John Wesley saw its potential and became a staunch supporter. Had Raikes endeavored to establish Sunday Schools at some other point in history, there is doubt that he would have seen lasting success.

Changes in Form and Content

As the Sunday School grew in England, a number of changes took place in its form and content. While the early pattern included paying the teachers a small sum for their services, teaching soon became a voluntary activity. By 1885 some teachers declined to accept payment for teaching. As more and more wealthy persons taught, the salary became less significant, until shortly after the turn of the century, teachers generally served without pay.

Another change that came about was in the curriculum of the schools. Initially, the Bible was the text, with few other resources available. The growth of Sunday School societies, and later unions, promoted the development of literature including spelling books and other publications. Early lessons included a strong emphasis on memorization. This trend increased greatly when Sunday Schools were established in the United States. Over a period of time, lessons included systematic Bible study, with a curriculum designed to be taught in weekly lessons.

The first schools taught all of the children together, regardless of their age or sex. Some of the difficulties encountered in early attempts grew out of this wide age and interest span. Eventually, students were graded by age, frequently with separate classes for boys and girls. Many of these developments will be considered more fully as we examine the Sunday School and its growth in the United States.

Rapid Growth

The Sunday School movement grew because of, and often times in spite of, its early policies and procedures. While it is difficult to identify the precise causes for growth, there is no question that there was growth, exceeding both imagination and definition. At the beginning of the movement in 1780, Raikes established four schools which ministered to a total of 90 children. Within four years after the 1783 announcement in the Gloucester *Journal,* Raikes claimed an enrollment of more than 250,000 pupils.

By the way of comparison, the Methodist movement should be considered. In the entire 50 years from the beginning of Wesley's revivals to the time of Raikes, a total of about 50,000 persons joined the Methodist organization. In just seven years from the Sunday School's beginning, the enrollment was over five times that many. Those denominations that supported and adopted Sunday Schools benefited from this general growth. One such denomination was the Methodist Church. When a strong emphasis on preaching and evangelism was coupled with the Sunday School instruction, the great blessing of God became evident.

In a report issued in 1835, after about 50 years of the Sunday School's existence, there were more than one and a half million students enrolled in the United Kingdom Sunday Schools. Of this total, over half of them attended no other school; Sunday School was their only educational experience. There were about 160,000 volunteer teachers instructing these pupils. This was an excellent student/teacher ratio of fewer than ten to one. In one Manchester school, there were more than 2,700 students with 120 unsalaried teachers. The amazing fact about this school was that all but three of those teachers themselves had been taught in Sunday Schools.

There were two noteworthy individuals whose ministries coincided with Raikes' work. Their combined efforts extended the results greatly beyond the best that each could have accomplished individually. John Wesley was one of these men. The evangelistic ministry that he and his preachers conducted made a vital contribution to Sunday School growth. The other man who played a vital role was William Fox.

William Fox

Curiously, Fox and Raikes were born on the same day in 1736. William Fox was a London merchant who recognized the same problems in England that Raikes saw. He perceived the moral decay and the physical and spiritual condition of the lower classes. As his business took him throughout England, he saw widespread spiritual and intellectual illiteracy. He was convinced that the only way England could be transformed was for the common man to learn and apply the principles of the Word of God. He knew, however, that merely owning copies of the Bible would do little good, for fewer than five percent of the population was able to read.

Like Raikes, Fox was an activist. He determined that he would work to help remedy the situation. And like Raikes, he had a group of friends who tried to discourage him. They told him the job was too big. They said that Fox would not be able to accomplish anything substantial. It was their conclusion that nothing short of an act of Parliament could bring about a change in the system. And, like Raikes, Fox chose to ignore their negativism. He was convinced that something had to be done, that it could be done, and that he could do it.

William Fox called together a group of influential friends who shared his vision and were willing to work with him. Together, they formed an organization to teach the common people to read, so that every person would become sufficiently literate to read the Bible for himself.

It is difficult to say what would have been the outcome of this group had Fox and his friends continued alone, since very early in the life of the organization, Fox heard of the work being done through Sunday Schools. He immediately saw the wisdom in Raikes' approach and agreed that Sunday instruction was more appropriate than the weekday instruction that he had suggested. With a humility and wisdom rarely seen today, Fox determined that rather than competing with Raikes and the Sunday School movement, he would join with them and cooperate in seeing his vision accomplished through Sunday Schools.

In September of 1785 Fox organized "The Society for the Support and Encouragement of Sunday Schools in the Different Counties of England." The purpose of the Society was to help in founding Sunday Schools, to provide the printed resources needed in these schools, and to raise money to help pay the expenses. With the contacts that Fox had, he was able to enroll a significant number of wealthy contributors. It was for this first fund-raising drive that Queen Charlotte headed the subscription list.

For nearly 20 years the Society furnished Bibles and Testaments, and paid teachers' salaries for Sunday Schools in England and Wales. In those years it assisted more than 2,500 schools, with almost a quarter of a million students. Society workers distributed nearly 250,000 spelling books, over 50,000 New Testaments, and more than 7,000 Bibles. Eventually, the Society was disbanded due to lack of funds.

London Sunday School Union

As a replacement for the Society, the London Sunday School Union was founded in 1803. The Union had a similar but not identical purpose. It helped to form new schools, secure buildings where the schools could meet, provide equipment, and supply financial loans or grants when improvements were needed. A major difference between the Society and the Union was that the Union discontinued paying the teachers. Instead, the money was used to prepare and publish periodical literature and needed books.

The man who was instrumental in founding the Union was William Gurney. He recognized that since Sunday School started as a charity movement, there was no standardization, and the schools ranged in quality from excellent to terrible. He wanted to improve their quality and to promote a more systematic approach to the organization and administration of the schools. By 1805, just two years after its organization, the Union had published four resources for Sunday Schools. These were, *A Plan for Forming Sunday Schools, A Guide to Teachers, A Catechism in Verse,* and *A Reading Primer.* The

London Sunday School Union set a pattern that the subsequent unions would follow, where teachers would serve unpaid and the Union would underwrite the extension of schools and the production of literature. While Robert Raikes is recognized for his vision in initiating the Sunday School movement, William Fox played a vital role in designing the organizational structure to help the movement grow beyond infancy.

John Wesley

The other man who played a strategic role in the development of Sunday Schools was John Wesley. Even before his conversion, John Wesley was a deeply religious man. In his early days at Oxford, Wesley was the leader of a small group of men (perhaps 25) known as the "Holy Club." Because of their disciplined ways, they became known as "Methodists." Out of this group came the Methodist movement, and later the Methodist denomination.

John Wesley had a deep compassion for people. As he was trying to express his desire to serve, a group of Moravian missionaries made a profound impact on him. Because of their ministry, Wesley subsequently surrendered his life to Christ, and was able to endure many difficulties and problems that would have overwhelmed a lesser man. About 40 years before Raikes opened his first Sunday School, Wesley began his ministry in earnest. Since he was not allowed to preach in the Church of England, at the urging of George Whitefield, Wesley turned to open air preaching. He declared, "The world is my parish!"

Wesley didn't want to withdraw from the Church of England, but he felt there were many things lacking in the church. One of these was evangelism. He organized groups of men to go out as itinerant evangelists. They traveled through all of the towns and villages of England, preaching and teaching the Word. Probably the best known of these preachers was George Whitefield. Both Wesley and Whitefield ministered effectively to the lower classes of society—those ordinarily excluded from formal religious activities.

Wesley was skilled in preaching, though not quite as eloquent as Whitefield. Wesley was an intense man with a gift for organization and an ability to motivate his followers. He wrote numerous books and used the substantial income from them to finance many philanthropic projects.

One of Wesley's deep concerns was to minister to children. He loved children and knew that they, as well as their parents, needed to learn about God. He instructed his preachers, urging them to "spend an hour a week with the children, in every large town, whether you like it or not. Talk with them every time you see any at home. Pray in earnest for them" (Trumbull, *Yale Lectures,* p. 108).

Wesley also was concerned about what would happen to his converts. Following the Moravian pattern, he organized them into small bands of five to ten people. These bands or "societies" were for mutual instruction and encouragement.

Wesley instructed his preachers to give attention to the children in two specific ways. As soon as there were ten or more children in an area, the preachers were to form a society for instructing the children. He also challenged the preachers to instruct parents in how to teach and guide their children. Wesley felt that it was imperative to reach the children as well as the adults in the household.

However, the major weakness in the pattern established by both the Methodists and the Moravians was the lack of biblical content in the instruction. While there was instruction, it focused mainly on the experiential aspect of Christianity, without systematic instruction in the Word. These Methodists and Moravians emphasized the effect but gave too little time to studying the cause. It was here that the Sunday School movement filled a void in the growing ministry of the Methodists.

Shortly after Sunday Schools began, Wesley wisely included them in the Methodist structure. Many feel that this accelerated the growth of Methodism many times over what it would have been otherwise. The Methodists, as no other denomination, made Sunday School one of the key elements in their organization. There was a natural integration for several reasons. Raikes and Wesley were both working within the same segment of English society. The miners, factory workers, and other laborers responded well to both ministries. Both strongly emphasized the Bible. The Methodists stressed evangelism, and Sunday Schools provided instruction for the converts. By combining their emphases, both organizations benefited and strengthened each other.

Contributions to England

At this point let's pause and consider the significant contributions that Sunday School made to England and the world. In a subsequent chapter we will evaluate its contribution to the United States. It is safe to say that Sunday School and its related ministries redirected the course of England. This influence can be observed in at least five categories.

• The Sunday School movement played a vital role in a spiritual awakening such as the world has rarely seen. Millions of people were influenced directly, and everyone was influenced, at least indirectly. One English historian claimed that the Sunday School movement, along with the revival stimulated by the ministries of Wesley and Whitefield, spared England from the horrors of the French Revolution (Clarence H. Benson, *A Popular History of Christian Education,* Moody Press, 1943, p. 128). When citizens were tranformed on the inside, they readily made changes on the outside and improved the conditions around them. Far more was accomplished through spiritually awakened persons who were committed to serving God than ever could have been accomplished through violence and revolution.

• A second outgrowth of the Sunday School movement was the stimulus to provide free education for all classes in society. Previously, education had been for the privileged few, but it became obvious that there was a better way. Not only were people happier and more fulfilled when they were educated, but they also became better workers and citizens. Rather than stimulating rebellion, education encouraged constructive solutions to society's problems. The English historian Green wrote, "The Sunday Schools established by Mr. Raikes of Gloucester were the beginning of popular education *(Ibid.,* p. 128). Others such as Lord Mahon and W.E.H. Lecky agreed with Green's conclusion that Sunday Schools had transformed English society.

• A third consequence of the Sunday School movement was that it awakened the upper and middle classes to their responsibility to other levels of society. But even more than that, it gave them a specific way to express their concern. They could become personally involved in organizing and teaching classes. They also could contribute financially to the expenses of such ministry.

The friends of William Fox said that what he wanted to do could be accomplished only by an act of Parliament. Raikes, Fox, Wesley, and others found a better way—one that went far beyond what Parliament possibly could have effected, or even expected. Ellwood Cubberley claimed that the Sunday School movement not only awakened in the lower classes a desire for educational reform, but also stimulated the upper and middle classes to recognize their responsibility to bring about educational and social reform.

• A fourth benefit was the production of religious literature needed for world evangelization. Organizations soon were established for the purpose of producing and distributing religious literature. Bible and tract societies and other groups responded to the need by writing and producing literature. While some was of mediocre or poor quality, the materials were generally well-done and used effectively. In just 20 short years after its founding, the Sunday School movement had extended around the world, and was playing a vital role in evangelizing almost all major countries.

• Finally, the Sunday School movement awakened and stimulated a desire for the education of adults. Although Raikes wanted to minister to adults, he had to forsake this desire and redirect his attention toward children. However, out of the children's emphasis, more adults were reached than he could have imagined teaching in the slums of Gloucester. By 1789 some adults were attending Sunday Schools, and very early in the Sunday School movement in Wales, adult ministry became a vital and continuing element.

There is no question that God enabled Robert Raikes to influence his contemporaries, and those who followed him, in a way that few men have been able to do. God's man doing God's work, in God's time, accomplished God's will. Robert Raikes was such a man. At his death in 1811, there were well over 400,000 Sunday School students in England. His funeral could well have been the funeral of a king, for the common folk mourned him in a special outpouring of love and affection. And as he had instructed in his will, each child attending his funeral received one shilling and a plum cake.

4
Across the Atlantic and into the Church

Most of the institutions that played a significant role in the early history of the United States were imported from Europe. Sunday School was no exception. However, while the citizens of the United States borrowed freely from more established nations, rarely was it done without making many adaptations. When a new nation is born, with no established traditions to guide it, traditions of those coming from other countries are called upon to fill in the gap. The blend of various backgrounds produces a cultural potpourri. This combines with a unique physical and social environment to produce a set of personalized institutions. Sunday School certainly was one of these American adaptations.

The Sunday School movement in North America began in the English tradition, with an emphasis on both moral and educational values. Teachers often received pay for their labors. Sunday School leaders also were deeply involved in the crusade for free public education, regardless of the child's social class. This parallel to English Sunday Schools didn't last long, however.

One of the unique features of American Sunday Schools was the variety of forms they took. The Sunday Schools of the South were different from those of the Northern and Middle States. Indeed, for many years there were no Sunday Schools to speak of in the North. The strong religious emphasis of the public school system somewhat reduced the need and the motivation to begin Sunday Schools. When

Sunday Schools finally were started in the Middle States, they were established primarily in the cities for the same reasons as in England.

Educational historian David B. Tyack wrote that philanthropists brought the English invention of the Sunday School to the United States (*Turning Points in American Education,* Blaisdell, 1967, p. 120). The Sunday School first gave secular instruction to the children who worked in factories, but rapidly it changed into a tool of the evangelical Protestant churches. Such a change never really occurred in England. Throughout the years of its development, the English Sunday School remained a lay movement, generally functioning outside of the institutional church. We will explore reasons for the differences between British and United States Sunday Schools in this chapter.

In its early days in the United States, Sunday School functioned as an extra-church agency. It was staffed by laymen, and often viewed with suspicion or fear by church leaders, who saw it as a British invention. Many church leaders did not actively oppose the Sunday School. More often they tolerated or ignored it.

However, as in England, the Sunday School grew, and grew phenomenally. The impact that Sunday School has had in North America, while not exactly the same as in England, is both profound and lasting. Let's consider how the Sunday School developed in this country and the role it has played in our moral and educational history.

The South

The earliest records of Sunday School in this country indicate that it began in the South, where the education of poor young people was given through apprenticeship programs. There were no state-supported schools as in the North, nor were there the strong parochial schools of the Middle States. It was the responsibility of the parents to provide basic education as best they could. To do this, wealthy parents ordinarily would hire teachers to come to their plantations to teach their children. But such instruction did not include lower-class children. And the children of slaves rarely were allowed to become apprentices.

William Elliott, a plantation owner in Accomac County on the

Eastern Shore of Virginia, was concerned for all of the children on his plantation. Early records indicate that he established the first Sunday School in this country on his plantation. The school met in his living room where he instructed both white and black children of those working on his plantation, but in segregated classes. He taught them to read and to study the Bible. He would read a portion of the Word, explain what it meant, and then encourage the children to memorize the Scripture. This school began in 1785 (just two years after Raikes' announcement in England) and continued in Elliott's home until 1801, when it was relocated in the church building. It became part of the church program, directed by church leaders, just 17 years later.

The Methodists

The Methodists in America knew of the success of Sunday Schools in England. Very quickly, they included Sunday School as a vital part of their church programming. Francis Asbury, the first bishop of the Methodist Church in the United States, learned about Sunday Schools from John Wesley. Asbury helped to establish the second Sunday School in this country. It was also located in Virginia, at the home of Francis Crenshaw in Hanover County. The purpose of this school was to teach the children of slaves.

It is difficult to separate the growth of Methodism from the growth of the Sunday School movement in this country. The founding and support of Sunday Schools was a key element in the extension program of the Methodist Church.

The Methodist conference in Charleston, South Carolina issued a resolution in 1790 calling for the establishment of Sunday Schools. The following resolution was a clear indication of the acceptance that the churches would give Sunday Schools. "Let us labor as the heart and soul of one man to establish Sunday Schools in or near the places of public worship. Let persons be appointed by the bishops, elders, deacons, or preachers to teach all that will attend and have capacity to learn from six o'clock in the morning until ten and from two o'clock in the afternoon until six, when it does not interfere with public worship. Be it further resolved that the council should compile a proper schoolbook to teach them learning and piety" (Benson, *Popular History,* p. 132).

This resolution indicates several distinguishing features of the future Sunday School. It was recognized as a program for which the church was responsible. It was to be scheduled so as to complement, not compete with, other church programs. It was to be available to all who would come. Also, there was a recognized need for proper curriculum materials to help accomplish the dual purpose of intellectual and spiritual instruction. These elements proved to be a common theme as Sunday Schools developed in this country.

The North

Conditions were different in the Northern States, and so the progress of Sunday School followed a somewhat different path. There was a strong system of state-supported, free public schools. The purpose in founding many of these was specifically religious in nature. It is clear from reading the Massachusetts education laws of 1647 and 1648, written nearly 150 years before the first United States Sunday School, that public schools had a distinct emphasis on religious instruction (Tyack, *Turning Points,* pp. 14-16).

The framers of these laws wrote in 1647, "It being one chief project of that old deluder Satan to keep men from the knowledge of Scripture . . ." In every township where there are fifty or more householders, they ". . . shall then forthwith appoint one from within their town to teach all such children as shall resort to him to write and read . . ." (*Ibid.,* pp. 14-16).

The following year another law was passed to appoint overseers who would make sure that the parents sent their children to the schools to be taught or otherwise made sure they were taught. The citizens had a deep commitment to the importance of education in cultivating intellectual and spiritual growth. Since the schools had been providing religious instruction, Sunday Schools were less needed in the North than in the South. When they *were* established, often it was to minister to children in the industrial context, as in England.

While religious instruction in school seemed to be a positive feature of the Northern States, actually such instruction generated problems. After the United States Constitution was adopted, the principle of separation of church and state left a void in the spiritual training of children. This was a gap that the churches of the North were not filling. H. Clay Trumbull, a staunch supporter of Sunday Schools, and early editor of *The Sunday School Times,* spoke to this matter in his series of lectures on the Sunday School at Yale University in 1888.

Trumbull said that preaching became much more popular than teaching because, "It is so much easier, on the one hand, to preach than it is to teach; and on the other hand, to hear than it is to learn; it is so much easier to tell what one knows or thinks, or what one thinks he knows, than it is to find out another's spiritual lack and need and capabilities, and to endeavor to supply them wisely . . ." (*Yale Lectures,* p. 76). He felt that the great pressures of pastoral responsibility and the emphasis on preaching (which he also supported) led to neglect of the children. Because of this, children received the form of religion, and went through all of the church activities, but often failed to perceive the reality and application of spiritual truth.

The Middle States

In parts of the Middle States, the social context was similar to England. The Industrial Revolution that stimulated the growth of cities, also helped to generate the same social conditions which made the Sunday School so needed in England. There were no free public schools, and children were subjected to long hours of hard labor. Their educational and moral needs were rarely cared for. Vice and immorality ran rampant in the towns and cities. While there were some scattered efforts to minister to children through Sunday Schools, these efforts were of limited impact due to the lack of a coordinated program.

The ravages of the Revolutionary War were sorely felt. There were few clergymen, and those who were ministering emphasized preaching and catechetical instruction. Many times this instruction fell far short of the creative discussion that Luther and others expected to arise from the question/answer format. Formality and rote memory were stressed more than understanding, so children often repeated meaningless words and phrases—if they received any instruction at all. Some felt that the only solution to this dilemma was intensive, purposeful Bible study, that would include relevancy rarely found in catechetical instruction.

After learning of the coordinated efforts characterizing English Sunday Schools, a group of citizens from Philadelphia organized the "First Day or Sabbath School Society." This Society was founded in 1790 for the purpose of instructing people and teaching them "from the Bible" and "from such other moral and religious books as the Society might, from time to time, direct" (Eavey, *Christian Education,* p. 232).

The organizers were concerned about the moral and religious character of the children, and also wanted to teach them to read and write. This group of laymen was organized to promote Sunday School apart from specific denominational ties. They had a significant ministry to the underprivileged and strongly supported the free public school concept.

Union Is Power

In 1817 the "Philadelphia Sunday and Adult School Union" was founded which led to the "American Sunday School Union," established in 1820. The vision of the founders can be seen through one of their mottoes, "Union Is Power." They felt that the efforts of regional Sunday School societies could have a far greater impact, and could accomplish far more, if the societies were coordinated. As the Union organized, it drew societies from all across the developing nation. Together, the members accomplished far more than they ever could have achieved alone, and more than even the most visionary leader could have anticipated.

The founders stated that they wanted to provide strength, experience greater efficiency through combined efforts, and save expense. In the first issue of the Union's periodical, *The American Sunday School Magazine,* published in 1824, the leaders stated that their purpose was to bind together ". . . the principal societies in the United States." This they did very well, as the central agency of Sunday School development and expansion in this country for well over 40 years.

The purpose of the Union as stated in its constitution was, "To concentrate the efforts of Sabbath-School Societies in the different sections of our country; to strengthen the hands of the friends of religious instruction on the Lord's Day; to disseminate useful information, circulate moral and religious publications in every part of the land, and to endeavor to plant a Sunday School wherever there is a population" (*The American Sunday School Magazine,* 1, no. 1, July 1824, p. 8).

American Sunday School Union
Growing out of this purpose were two great emphases of the American Sunday School Union. First, the Union took the lead in writing and producing Sunday School literature. It also labored diligently to establish and encourage Sunday Schools all across the land. In the next chapter we shall consider the work of the best known missionary of the Union, Stephen Paxson.

A distinctive feature of the Union was that it began and was structured to continue as a lay organization. The founders were not opposed to clergymen—indeed, the outstanding pastors of the 19th century were called upon to address the conventions. But the framers of the American Sunday School Union constitution were convinced that laymen could promote a cooperative effort that would extend beyond denominational loyalties. That constitution permitted only laymen to serve as officers, in order to insure the lay direction considered important to the Sunday School's success.

The effort that was conceived of as national in scope soon became just that. A report published in *The American Sunday School Magazine* in 1824 indicated that within those few short years, the societies in union extended from Massachusetts to Tennessee, and from New Jersey to Missouri. Seventeen states were represented in this early roll call of members.

Another report in the same issue described the growth of Sunday Schools in this country between 1818 and 1824. In 1818 there were 43 schools, while by 1824, the number had grown to 723. In those same six years the number of teachers jumped from 556 to 7,300. The combined total of teachers and students increased by more than 50,000 in those years. The growth of the American Sunday School Union represents the expansion of the Sunday School movement in the United States.

The unique political circumstances in the United States created special problems for the Sunday School. There was a need to instruct children in religion and morals, due to the constitutional mandate to keep functions of the church and school separate. Unfortunately, the church was ill-prepared to provide such instruction. So the Sunday School stepped in to fill this gap, and instructed the children so effectively that soon the Sunday School became an arm of the church. The emphasis on biblical instruction became the predominant theme of the Sunday School in this country.

With a quality public school system, the necessity for teaching reading and writing was minimized. This enabled the leaders of the Sunday School movement to concentrate their efforts on spiritual instruction. For a number of years, however, the Sunday Schools in the newly settled regions of the country included basic reading and writing skills in the curriculum, until other educational institutions assumed responsibility for these services.

Purpose of the Sunday School

Perhaps the American Sunday School Union can be taken as the best spokesman for the purpose of the Sunday School. In describing the function of the Sunday School, the Union wrote in 1824 that the single great end of all religious teaching is, ". . . to guide perishing souls to Christ for salvation."

To assume that this was a simplistic purpose would be false. The leaders of the Union understood the implications of Christian living that are recognized today by Christian educators. In the *American Sunday School Magazine,* a more comprehensive explanation was given of the purpose of Sunday Schools: "Their object, which has often been stated, and must be generally known, is to teach, on the Lord's Day, all classes of persons, who may avail themselves of the privilege, to read and understand the Bible; and to invite them to the practice of its precepts" (*Ibid.,* p. 3).

In this broader statement of purpose, several things are important. The purpose of Sunday School emphasized biblical instruction for all social classes. The purpose of the instruction was to help the students practice biblical principles. Sunday Schools were to help people learn what God had said, so that they could live as He wanted them to live.

While the Sunday School emphasis in England included basic educational skills for many years, such instruction in reading and writing was de-emphasized in American Sunday Schools. As a matter of record, the American Sunday School Union wanted to keep religious instruction out of the public schools, preferring that the church and Sunday School teach the Bible. Leaders stated that even when formal education of children was provided, Sunday Schools still were needed. "Their aid would then be required to make the young thoroughly acquainted with the Word of God; because, although the good old custom of reading the Scriptures at the beginning and close of school still obtains in some places; yet, generally, the Bible is a book almost wholly excluded from our common schools; and if read at all, rarely with the solemn reverence and fixed attention which become an assembly of young immortals, when they consult the Oracles of God" (*Ibid.,* pp. 2-3).

Trumbull defined the main elements of a Sunday School in his Yale lectures of 1888. He stated that the source of authority of the Sunday School was the church. The subject matter was the Bible and the teaching method, discussion. Laymen were to teach children, in small classes, with all of the classes being grouped under one common head. Such characteristics are descriptive of many Sunday Schools even today.

Changes

The curriculum and methods of Sunday School instruction underwent significant change over the years. When the first American Sunday Schools were established, they had a crude trial-and-error curriculum. Generally, all of the children were lumped together, with little thought given to classifying them. While the teachers had good motivations and were godly individuals, they were poorly trained and ill-prepared for their task. It is important, however, to realize that they made an impact and ministered to children. Sunday School was far from perfect, but it helped accomplish the mission of the church.

• Previously, the catechism was the usual starting point for classes in religious education. Sunday School leaders chose instead to emphasize the Bible. If any single factor were to be identified as the main characteristic of early Sunday Schools, it should be the emphasis on *instruction from the Bible.* The Bible was the textbook. There was an attempt to combine the catechetical method and Bible knowledge. Often the question/answer format was encouraged to help students learn Bible facts. This was especially important since so few persons had an accurate knowledge of Bible content.

• The emphasis on content led to a *natural focus on memorization.* Many have cited the excesses in this approach, and have depreciated the value of early Sunday Schools. It is true that some children learned hundreds or thousands of verses, often at random. It is true that many of the class sessions were totally consumed by the recitation of these verses. It is true that children often memorized out of a strong competitive urge, or to earn the colorful tickets that could be redeemed for prizes such as books and Bibles.

But it is also true that the Word of God was implanted deep in the minds and hearts of young people. When few could read well, and fewer still had books of their own, many children grew up with a vast knowledge of Bible facts. Facts that could be applied to life when needed. Facts that the Holy Spirit could bring back to their memories at some later point in their lives.

• When the emphasis on memorizing the catechism at the very beginning of the Sunday School movement gave way to memorizing Bible verses, it was natural that some sort of system should be established to *organize instruction.* By the 1820s the leaders of the American Sunday School Union were encouraging the study of selected passages of Scripture. These were frequently 10-20 verses in length. The class session often consisted of reading (and memorizing) the passage, followed by a discussion of its meaning and application.

• By about 1830 one of the key contributions of the Union was begun. The need for literature and teachers' helps was obvious, so the American Sunday School Union developed a fairly *uniform lesson series* to be used in all Sunday Schools. The Union also published, and periodically updated, booklets of "Union Questions" that were prepared for the teachers and students to use. Other aids and resources were prepared regularly to further assist the teachers.

One historian, E. Morris Fergusson, wrote about the valuable resources provided through the American Sunday School Union publications. Through successive issues of Scripture question books, with the excellent Bible dictionaries and other helps that formed part of the system, the Union strongly contributed to the development and supply of the Sunday School's curriculum (*Historic Chapters in Christian Education,* Fleming H. Revell, 1935, pp. 24-25).

Five Distinctive Characteristics

Before considering the ministry of the most significant Sunday School pioneer in this country, let's pause and briefly consider some of the features of Sunday Schools as they developed in this country. While many of these could be recognized in other countries also, these qualities strongly characterized American Sunday Schools.

• Sunday School quickly became a ministry of the church. While initially it was promoted independently of the church, by the early 1800s it was widely accepted as an arm of the church, although this is not to imply that *all* pastors gladly welcomed Sunday Schools in their churches.

Some pastors opposed it outright. One Connecticut pastor is supposed to have said, while brandishing his cane toward a Sunday School class meeting on the church steps, "You imps of Satan doing the devil's work, I'll have you set in the street" (Eavey, *Christian Education,* p. 233). Pastors such as this refused even to allow classes to meet in the church.

Some were a bit more tolerant and rented space to Sunday Schools so that the classes could meet. Others grudgingly permitted classes to be held in the church, but with vehement assertions that it was against their better judgment. For the most part, however, pastors and other church leaders perceived the value of Sunday Schools and even encouraged their organization.

• A second characteristic of the American Sunday School, in addition to becoming part of the local church, was that there was great concern that the Sunday School not usurp the role of parents in instructing their children. In one of its early publications, the American Sunday School Union ominously stated, "It is not the office of a Sabbath School teacher to do the work which belongs to the parents of his pupils, though he may assist them. We have no wish to relieve parents of their awful charge; we rather wish they may feel loaded with a burden which, as long as they live, they cannot lay upon another" (*The American Sunday School Magazine,* p. 3).

The Union leaders stated three key problems that they wished to deal with; the relationship with parents was one. The leaders were concerned about quality teachers, facilities, and about not usurping parents' responsibilities. The man whom we shall consider in the next chapter, Stephen Paxson, clearly demonstrated this concern in his ministry.

• A third characteristic of the Sunday School movement in this country was the emphasis on children. While in other countries adults were often included—an emphasis of the Sunday Schools in Wales— this usually was not done in the United States. In this country adults sometimes attended, but more by chance than by design.

• A fourth characteristic was the variety of types of Sunday Schools that developed. While Sunday Schools started on the English plan, because of the nature and diversity of American life, several other forms soon became evident. One of these was the church Sunday School that has become most common. The church Sunday School was organized as a program for the members of a given church. In this form, children, and later adults, came to receive Bible instruction in the church where they regularly worshiped.

However, two other styles also developed. One of these was the mission Sunday School. This frequently was organized by a church or group of laymen who wished to minister in the city to a class of youngsters ordinarily neglected by the church. This form closely resembled the early English Sunday School. The other style was the pioneer Sunday School. The pioneer Sunday School often assumed the entire responsibility for evangelism, instruction, worship and most other functions of spiritual leadership. The pioneer Sunday School was common along the developing frontiers of this country. It was into these areas that the American Sunday School Union sent pioneer missionaries. No other institution took such responsibility for the educational and spiritual development of the pioneers living on the edges of our nation as did the Sunday School.

• The fifth characteristic of the American Sunday School was its nonaristocratic character. In many parts of the world, Sunday School was viewed as something the upper class did for—and sometimes to—the lower class. There were clear-cut distinctions between classes. In the United States, this concept was rejected and actively opposed.

The well-known and eloquent preacher, Dr. Lyman Beecher, wanted to avoid any social class distinction in Sunday School. He convinced both a judge and an aristocratic lady to send their children to Sunday School with his children. He wanted to encourage all classes of children to attend Sunday School. He said, "I have made up my mind to take my children, and I want you and a few others of the best families to popularize the thing" (Fergusson, *Historic Chapters,* pp. 26-28).

While there is no question that the concept of Sunday School as we know it was imported from England, there is also little question that it adapted and grew with a life of its own after being transplanted. Even as it was part of a worldwide movement, the Sunday School became a distinctive American institution that has been profoundly influencing this country for almost 200 years.

5
A Man, a Horse,
and a Sunday School

Imagine, if you will, a 30-year-old man, partially crippled, who has such a severe speech impediment that he was unable to receive formal education. Think of this man living in the 1800s on the American frontier with no transportation other than foot or horseback. The roads on which he travels are often rocky patches connected by mudholes. This hostile environment is home to hostile Indians, and even hostile settlers.

Imagine this man traveling hundreds of thousands of miles in almost 40 years of service, founding or helping to organize more than 3,000 Sunday Schools. Think of him as the most important single influence in evangelizing the American frontier. Picture a man who is as much at home in Big Muddy as in Boston, who can communicate with people equally well in Mosquito Creek or Philadelphia. Think of this man who didn't accept Christ until he was well into his 30s. His name is Stephen Paxson.

Apostle to the Children

If such a description were written as fiction, most of us would reject it as being implausible, too far-fetched. And yet these are but a few characteristics of Stephen Paxson, the unique individual who is the best known, and perhaps most influential, of all Sunday School workers in the history of the United States. Paxson came to be known

as both "The Children's Preacher" and "The Apostle to the Children."
H. Clay Trumbull eulogized him in this way: "Stephen Paxson is
perhaps more peculiarly and emphatically to be taken as a representative product and promoter of the pioneer Sunday School of America
than any man who has lived; and because of this fact, if for no other,
his story ought not to pass out of mind with his passing away from
active labor among us" (B. Paxson Drury, *A Fruitful Life,* American
Sunday School Union, 1882, p. 214).

Even while he was alive, other leaders of the Sunday School
movement recognized the significant impact that Paxson was
making. A tribute written in the *National Sunday School Teacher*
asserted, "When the history of the Sunday School movement of
today comes thoroughly to be written, his name will stand in shining
characters as having no mean part in it" *(Ibid.* p. 173).

Beginning by Accident

Since Paxson came to Christ through the Sunday School, it was
logical that he should have such a passion for this work. As a child he
was severely crippled in one foot. This condition caused him
discomfort and pain throughout his life. Also, a speech impediment
made it so difficult for him to speak that an impatient teacher gave up
in disgust and refused to allow him to attend school. What little
education he received, he gave to himself. As a very moral man in his
30s, Paxson was a good husband and father. He was fairly successful
in his chosen vocation and felt that he had little need for church or
religion.

Because of his deep love for and commitment to his daughter,
Paxson reluctantly agreed to accompany her to Sunday School one
Sunday. She had promised to bring a visitor and had no one left to
turn to but her father. He consented to go with her, planning to leave
as soon as her obligation had been fulfilled. After all, adults didn't
attend Sunday School at that time.

When he entered the school, he addressed several men: "Gentle-
men, now tell me what you do here." The superintendent replied, "We
have a union Sunday School. I'm a Methodist, Mr. Carter is a
Presbyterian, Mr. Miner here is a Baptist, but we all unite to study the
Bible." Paxson's daughter later wrote, "This remark pleased him

also, for he had heard very little about churches except their quarrels and dissensions" *(Ibid., p. 35).*

Since the teacher of a boys' class hadn't shown up that morning, Paxson was conscripted to supervise the class. The boys told him the procedure, how to ask the questions and find the answers, how to supervise the memory work and give the tickets as rewards, and the other components of a Sunday School lesson. At the end of the session, Paxson felt embarrassed at his ignorance and lack of skill. He vowed to return the next week, prepared to do a better job.

It wasn't until Stephen Paxson had been attending and instructing for four years that he decided to personally accept Jesus Christ. Because of his deep appreciation for what God had done in his life, and because of his enthusiasm for Sunday School, he left his trade as a hatter a few years later. Selling their house in Winchester, Illinois, the Paxson family moved to Pike County. There they lived in a log cabin on Hickory Hill, so that they could survive on Paxson's dollar-a-day salary as a missionary of the American Sunday School Union.

A Determined Man

In spite of his lameness and continual pain, Paxson had learned to walk without appearing to be uncomfortable. Determining to work on his severe speech problem with just as much diligence, he discovered a solution. By taking a deep breath and expelling it slowly—accompanied by descriptive hand gestures—he could speak. As this technique was developed, he became a colorful and exceedingly effective communicator.

The things that often stop other men seemed to call forth greater efforts from Paxson. He was willing to talk to both the cultured and the crude. He was as welcome in New York as in Loafer Prairie. One of his favorite expressions was, "Facts are God's arguments." And he shared these "facts" with all whom he met. Weather didn't bother him. He maintained, "A Sunday School born in a snowstorm will never be scared by a white frost." As a missionary commissioned in 1848, but serving even before then, he devoted his life to advancing the cause of Sunday School for almost 40 years.

Life in the prairie region covered by Paxson didn't include roads as we know them. Therefore, horseback was the only feasible means of transportation. And yet even by horseback, Paxson covered the territory from the Great Lakes to the Gulf, and from the Allegheny Mountains to the Rockies. He came to be recognized by most of the settlers in this region and was well-known by many. As a matter of fact, there were even some people who wished they could get away from him. Paxson told this story:

In a log schoolhouse, on the banks of the "Grand Chariton," in Missouri, after I had finished making a speech in favor of establishing a Sunday School, a plainly dressed farmer arose and said he would like to make a few remarks. I said, "Speak on, sir."

He said to the audience, pointing across the room at me, "I've seen that chap before. I used to live in Macoupin County, Illinois and that man came there to start a school. I told my wife that when Sunday Schools came around, game got scarce, and that I would not go to his school or let any of my folks go. It was not long before a railroad came along, so I sold out my farm for a good price and moved to Pike County. I hadn't been there more than six months before that same chap came to start a Sunday School.

"I said to my wife, 'That Sunday School fellow is about; so I guess we'd better move to Missouri.' Land was cheaper in Missouri, so I came and bought me a farm and went back for my family. I told them Missouri was a fine state, game plenty, and better than all, no Sunday School there.

"Day before yesterday, I heard that there was to be a Sunday School lecture at the schoolhouse by some stranger. Says I to my wife, 'I wonder if it can be possible that it is that Illinoisan!' I came here myself on purpose to see, and, neighbors, *it's the very same chap!*

"Now, if what he says about Sunday School is true, it's a better thing than I thought. If he has learned so much in Sunday School, I can learn a little, so I've just concluded to come to Sunday School and to bring my seven boys."

Putting his hand in his pocket, he pulled out a dollar, and coming to the stand where I was, laid it down, saying, "That'll help buy a library." Then he added, "Neighbors, if I should go to Oregon or California, I'd expect to see that chap there in less than a year."

Someone in the audience spoke up—"You are treed."

"Yes," he said, "I *am* treed at last. Now I am going to see this thing through, for if there is any good in it, I am going to have it" *(Ibid.,* pp. 72-74).

"Robert Raikes"

In order to travel so extensively, Paxson needed a rugged horse. His first horse was not up to the rigors of such a life and before long was completely disabled. A church in Pittsfield, Illinois took up an offering for a "Missionary Horse." With this money Stephen Paxson purchased a horse that he wryly named "Robert Raikes." "Robert Raikes" carried Paxson for 25 years, over more than 100,000 miles of the Midwest. Even the horse became well-known and loved, and was referred to by the children as "Dear Old Bob."

"Robert Raikes" came to know Paxson's habits so well that he automatically stopped whenever he came to a child, and turned in at every church and school. Paxson's daughter reported, "Once a young man borrowed Old Bob to take a young lady out riding. He moved along in good style till he met the children coming home from school, and then stopped. The driver told him to 'Get up,' but Bob would not move a peg. The young man flourished a whip, but Bob was evidently going to be obstinate. The children gathered around, much to the young man's discomfiture, but all at once he suspected what Bob was waiting for, so he made a little speech to the children, bade them 'Good-evening,' shook the lines, and passed on" *(Ibid.,* pp. 86-87).

A Horse Story

Paxson was a keen observer of human nature and a shrewd judge of how best to communicate with his listeners. He loved to relate tales of his experiences, and with his sharp memory, he would repeat long descriptions and extensive dialogue in precise detail. He had the knack of selecting exactly the right story to tell and of telling it in such a way as to charm his listeners. One of his favorite stories relates to his horse, "Robert Raikes," and demonstrates the impact of his ministry. Originally written by Paxson, this account was published in numerous Sunday School papers:

I drove up to a blacksmith's shop a few days since to get my horse shod. The blacksmith walked up to the horse and looked him square in the face, then turning to the people about said, "I have shod hundreds of horses, and have seen thousands, but there" (pointing to my horse) "is the best countenance and best shaped head I ever saw!"

While he was shoeing him, I made some inquiries concerning a Sabbath School, and told him my horse and myself were both missionaries. He immediately dropped the horse's foot, and, seating himself on the ground, said:

"Stranger, let me give you a little of my history. I was an orphan boy, bound out to learn the blacksmith's trade. My master would not send me to school, but kept me hammering hot iron day and night until I was 19 years old. About that time a Sunday School man came to the settlement, and went around, telling the people to come out, and he would start a Sunday School. So I got my day's work done and went to hear him. He told me a heap of good things, and among others that he himself first went to Sunday School when about 30 years old, and how much he learned and what a blessing it was to him.

"Now, thinks I, continued the blacksmith, *that's just my fix, and if he starts a school, I'll go.* A school was started, and I went for two years. I soon learned to read my Bible, and the very day I was 21, I joined the church of Christ. For seven years I have been trying to serve Him. Last Sunday I was made the superintendent of a school here."

I asked him where the school was, in which he learned to read and was converted to Christ.

"Oh! More than 100 miles from here," he replied.

He gave me the name and all the particulars of its organization. I then asked him if he would know the man who organized that school. He did not know as he would, it had been so long ago, but recollected that he was large, almost as large as myself. I then informed him that I was the person, and that the horse was along too. He sprang to his feet, exclaiming "Blessed father, is it possible?"

While my hand rested in his, the tears rolled down his cheeks like rain. He said: "All that I am I owe under God to that school. There I learned to read and to love my blessed Saviour." He took me to his house and introduced me to his wife, a good Christian woman, the mother of two children.

When I offered to pay him, he said, "No; never a cent for shoeing the missionary horse! I will shoe him all his life for nothing, if you will bring him to me."

To you this may not be particularly interesting, but to me it was one of the most pleasing incidents in my life. I felt that the starting of that one school was worth a lifetime of toil *(Ibid.,* pp. 87-90).

"Robert Raikes, the Missionary Horse" served Paxson for more than 25 years, and was valued by him as a vital companion in his work. He served while Paxson founded more than 700 Sunday Schools. The fame of "Robert Raikes" was such that after he died, his story was distributed and read in every state of the Union. With 100 dollars given by a friend, Paxson was able to purchase a horse to carry on in the fine tradition of his predecessor. This horse was named "Robert Raikes, Junior."

Books for Sunday School

The passion of Stephen Paxson was to fulfill the mission of the American Sunday School Union. Union leaders had committed themselves to establishing a Sunday School in every community where there was none. In order to do this, Paxson traveled to the most remote and inaccessible corners of the Midwest. He would travel to a town, or even a small group of settlers. There he contacted everyone in the area, inviting them to a meeting. And in this meeting he would entertain them with his stories and challenge them with their responsibilities.

Founding a Sunday School consisted of securing a place where it could meet, getting one or more persons to agree to teach, and trying to persuade the local settlers to contribute enough to raise five dollars. For this amount, the American Sunday School Union would provide a library of more than 100 volumes worth more than ten dollars.

However, with the limited financial resources of many of the settlers, even five dollars was a difficult sum to raise. Paxson settled upon a method to handle this problem that even today would excite any door-to-door salesman. When the good folk of the community would indicate (as they often did) that they had no money until harvesttime, Paxson would ask, "But how much *would* you give toward buying a library, supposing you had the money?" Ordinarily those in attendance stated that they would give between five and fifteen dollars—if they had it.

"Now," replied Paxson, "is there not some gentleman present who would advance the sum these people are willing to pay for a library, and allow them to repay him at their earliest convenience?" Paxson reported that since there was usually at least one person better off than his neighbors, this almost always worked *(Ibid.,* p. 117).

Paxson was never a man to miss any opportunity to speak out for the cause of Sunday School. His daughter, B. Paxson Drury, wrote in his biography, *A Fruitful Life,* "that upon one occasion he came upon an immense Fourth of July mass meeting. He was soon called upon for a patriotic speech. 'That is not in my line,' he responded, 'but if you really wish to hear me, I will give you a Sunday School talk'" *(Ibid.,* p. 69). She further reported that soon he had the crowd cheering just as much for Sunday Schools as they had been cheering for the Declaration of Independence.

At the end of this speech, Paxson asked for a representative of each neighborhood lacking a Sunday School to come forward. He had the person give his name and the name of the schoolhouse in the area. The list of names that he accumulated included Cracker Bend, Mosquito Creek, Big Muddy, Hoosier Prairie, Loafer Grove, Stringtown, and Buckhorn. Only a few weeks passed before a Sunday School was established in every one of the 30 communities listed that day.

He was never afraid of hard work, and never daunted by the difficulties and discomfort he had to endure. On one occasion he reported founding 40 Sundays Schools in 40 days. The record of one a day was a feat next to impossible, given the conditions under which he was working. Paxson concluded his report of the incident by stating, "But I had to work day and night like a horse" *(Ibid.,* p. 161).

One of the abilities that greatly aided Stephen Paxson in his ministry was his unique skill in relating to all classes of society. He seemed to be as much at ease with the uneducated pioneer as with the business man or polished woman in large cities like Boston, New York, or Philadelphia. Even his grammatical blunders and missed pronounciations did not offend the cultured and refined, since his ideas were so refreshing and his communication so picturesque. The uneducated responded equally well to his colorful tales and homespun logic.

Peach Basket Speech

One of Paxson's favorite stories relates how he convinced a father to start his children in a local Sunday School. He wrote:

Upon one occasion I called upon a Mr. Allen, to ascertain his views in reference to organizing a Sunday School in his vicinity. I found him engaged in peeling peaches upon the back porch. He asked me to take a chair and help myself to the fruit. While we were eating the peaches, I began the conversation by asking him if there was a Sunday School in his neighborhood.

"No!" was the reply, "and, as for me, I am down on education! It only makes thieves and rascals of people."

I tried to show him that while a merely intellectual education might sometimes result in that way, such could never be the case were the education complete or threefold in its nature—physical, intellectual, and moral; that as his children's physical powers would be developed in consequence of their work upon their farm, their mental capacity would be enlarged and strengthened in the common schools. What they needed besides was a moral and religious culture in the Sunday School, where they would learn their duty to God and their obligations to man—that the moral education was of the utmost importance, and was what the Sunday School undertook to do for a child. I inquired how his children spent Sundays.

"Climb trees and wear out their duds," was the response.

"But," I inquired, "would it not be better, simply on the score of economy, for them to be in Sunday School instead of wearing out their clothes?"

"Well, p'r'aps it would," was the response. "How much will it cost to run it?"

"Nothing," I replied.

"What! Are you coming here to teach school for nothing?"

"No," I explained. "You know Mr. Green and wife, who live

above here; they have consented to take classes. How many children have you old enough to attend school?"

"Well! Let me see." He began counting on his fingers. He made a miscount. "Kitty! Kitty!" he called. "Come here, wife, and name over the children while I count; this man wants to know how many children we have old enough to go to Sunday School."

They made the number 13. I looked off to the meadow, and saw a drove of hogs feeding upon the clover.

"How many hogs have you over there?" I inquired.

"Eighty-three fine, fat fellows," he promptly responded.

"Now, see here, my friend; when I ask you how many children you have over five years of age, you are obliged to call your wife to help you count them; but when I ask you how many hogs you have, you answer without hesitation. Where, now, is your mind? Upon your children or upon your hogs?"

He looked up at me with a laugh and said, "I acknowledge, old hoss, you've got me; it's too much on the hogs!"

Two years afterward I called upon this farmer again. I found that he had joined the church, as had also two of his sons. He thanked me warmly for the change that had been wrought in his family by what he called my "peach basket speech" *(Ibid.,* pp. 78-80).

Paxson as Public Speaker

Paxson was such a skillful communicator that in the winter, when travel was too difficult in the Midwest, he often would travel through the East, speaking at assemblies in the major cities. In these meetings sponsored by the American Sunday School Union, he would receive offerings and pledges from those in attendance to extend the work of the Union. Frequently, thousands of dollars were raised in a single meeting.

Following one of these meetings in Boston, the newspaper reported, "At the close of the address a handsome collection was taken up to aid Mr. Paxson's missionary work in the West. Many persons remained to shake hands with one who had organized more than 1,000 Sabbath Schools, and an earnest desire was expressed to have him speak again in Boston. This he will probably do, as he speaks every night in the week save Saturday" *(Ibid.,* p. 108).

Following a meeting in New York, the report in the newspaper gave an indication of how enjoyable and effective a speaker Paxson was. "Last evening a meeting was held in Dr. Spring's church, corner of 37th Street and Fifth Avenue, in behalf of the American Sunday School Union.

"The indefatigable missionary, Stephen Paxson, made an address in which his aristocratic auditors were so deeply interested that they wept and smiled alternately, never heeding mistakes in grammar, or rhetorical discrepancies. They were assured that Mr. Paxson was just the man for the work. He has a good head, well-poised, over a heart filled with love for his noble task. He has accomplished a work that the most popular dignitary in the church might be proud to acknowledge. The contributions for this occasion were 5,000 dollars" *(Ibid.,* pp. 108-109).

A New York writer described Paxson's speech as "a model speech; short, pointed, racy, effective." The reporter added, "We need more such." He further wrote, "At times the audience was convulsed with laughter, and then the eye was dimmed with tears. Every story was told with inimitable effect" *(Ibid.,* p. 109).

An example of the sense of humor that pervaded all of his communication can be seen in the way he autographed a friend's Bible. Paxson wrote, "The essential elements of a Sabbath School are Grace, Grit, and Greenbacks—Stephen Paxson" *(Ibid.,* p. 200).

Personal Life

However, the same intensity and drive that enabled him to effectively extend Sunday Schools into the Midwest, often made him somewhat difficult to get along with. Perhaps no one perceived this any more than his friends. Just a few months before his death, Paxson said, "I have one more conquest to make, and then my life work is done. I must learn to be patient, and not to rebuke my friends for their blunders" *(Ibid.,* p. 179).

Paxson was also prone to leave his family for extended periods of time as he traveled in his ministry. The children were left in the capable care of his wife. Paxson's daughter wrote that her mother had a mystical ability to know when Paxson was arriving home, even to the extent of telling the children, and preparing for his arrival with the children sitting out on the fence to greet their father.

This is all the more amazing when we realize that there was no means of communication available, and often the trips lasted for weeks or months. On one occasion Paxson's return had been predicted by his wife, but she later revised the date by several days, saying that he was sick and had been detained. When he arrived on the revised date, Paxson told them he would have been there sooner, but that he had been delayed by sickness in southern Illinois. When asked once how she knew about his illness, Sarah Paxson replied that she didn't know how, but that she must have had a dream.

On another occasion the children were all ready for their father to return. When dark and bedtime came, the children retired, disappointed. Finally, at eleven o'clock he arrived, cold, muddy, and dripping wet. He stated that he thought he would keep on, "in spite of the wind and weather, for I was sure mother would be expecting me."

Heaven's Last Experiment

Stephen Paxson's life was characterized by an uncommon dedication to God and a conviction of the importance of an idea. The idea that generated this conviction was Sunday School. He once described Sunday School as, "heaven's last experiment to aid God's ministers in bringing the world to Christ" *(Ibid.,* p. 127). He never saw the church and Sunday School as competitive in any way. Indeed, many of his Sunday Schools soon grew into churches and called their own pastors. Often, these pastors were, themselves, products of Sunday Schools.

Paxson was convinced of the power of God's Word to transform lives. He proclaimed the value of Bible instruction wherever he went. He felt this was the best preparation that any child could have and didn't hesitate to say so. Sometimes this even got him into trouble with his listeners, such as one professor of religion whom he met.

Paxson related this account to demonstrate how valuable a Sunday School education could be.

I was once organizing a Sunday School, and, in the course of my remarks, I made the assertion that a child who had had the advantages of a Sunday School education knew more of the

Scriptures at 10 years of age than a young man of 20 did when I was young. After the meeting was over, a man said to me: "Did I understand you to say that a boy of 10 knows more now than a man of 20 used to?"

"No, my friend; I said a boy who has had the *advantages* of a Sunday School knows more at 10 about his Bible, than a young man of 20 knew when I was young."

"Well, I don't believe it, anyhow."

"I am sorry," I replied, "that there is no Sunday School scholar present to test it."

A lady standing by said: "There is a Sunday School scholar over at my house; he came just before the meeting."

"Come," I said. "We will find this boy and see."

He agreed to the proposal, and on our way over I inquired how old he was. He said, "Fifty years."

"How long have you been a professor of religion?"

"Thirty years," he replied.

"Now, my friend, if we find this boy, I will ask you some questions; and, if you don't answer them, have you any objection to the boy answering?"

"None, if they are fair questions."

"You need not answer them, if they are not."

Upon reaching the house we found a bright-eyed boy some 10 years of age. I asked him how long he had been a member of a Sunday School.

"Eighteen months," was the reply.

"Did you have a book in your Sunday School called the *Child's Scripture Question Book?*"

"Oh, yes! That was the first book I studied."

I knew then what questions to ask him. I said to the gentleman: "How many books are contained in the Old Testament?"

He studied awhile, and then said: "I give it up."

"Can you tell?" I asked the boy. He replied correctly.

I said to the gentleman, "Perhaps you have been a New Testament scholar; tell me how many books are contained in the New Testament?"

He began counting on his fingers, *Matthew, Mark, Luke, John,* and so on. He said the number 26.

"Is he right, my son?" I inquired of the boy.

"No, sir; there are 27."

"What is the first book in the Bible?" I asked the man. He responded, "Genesis."

I said, "Right; you have answered one to the boy's two. Now please give the definition of *genesis.*"

He replied, gruffly, "I never studied Dictionary."

I asked the boy. He replied, "I think it means 'creation' or 'beginning.'"

I took a Bible dictionary from my satchel and showed him that the boy was right; for otherwise he would not have believed either of us.

He sprang to his feet, exclaiming, "I understand you, sir; you have had this little shaver out in the hazel brush, training him to answer these questions."

I soon proved by the lady that I had never seen the child before. Then I handed him the Bible, and told him to ask the boy any question he saw fit. He soon threw down the book, saying: "Why, he knows more than I do at 50!"

I responded, "He is, perhaps, no smarter naturally than you were, but he has had advantages of which you and I never dreamed. There was no *Child's Scripture Question Book* in our school days. Truth had not been simplified to the comprehension of a child; your sole literature was *Dilworth's Spelling Book* and *Sindbad the Sailor,* while I had even less."

It is needless to add that the man was in favor of buying a Sunday School library, and so were all the audiences to whom the story was told *(Ibid.,* pp. 56-60).

Stephen Paxson, through his commitment to God and the Sunday School movement, had a profound impact in the frontiers of the United States, and also in the well-established eastern cities. While others may have had less impact due to lesser skills, nevertheless Paxson was only 1 of more than 100 such missionaries. His enthusiasm was so contagious that his eldest son, at age 15, joined his father in missionary work and went on to establish more than 700 Sunday Schools, himself.

This review of the diligence and faithfulness of Stephen Paxson's ministry is a testimony to the power of God working through one man. In almost 40 years of service, Stephen Paxson founded more than 1,300 Sunday Schools and assisted more than 1,700 others. It's impossible to document the number of persons who were led to Christ either directly or indirectly through his work. Just as Robert Raikes of Gloucester represents English Sunday Schools, so Stephen Paxson represents the impact of the Sunday School in America.

6
Transformation
of a Nation

During the middle and late 1800s, the Sunday School movement in the United States grew beyond all expectations. This was when Stephen Paxson, and others doing a similar job, extended the outreach of the American Sunday School Union into all parts of the country. The Union accomplished a task that had rarely been done— it secured cooperation from all of the major denominations. Rather than functioning autonomously, and competing with each other, these denominations looked to the Sunday School Union to bring them together and to help expand the ministry of the Sunday School.

Evangelical historian C.B. Eavey wrote that this cooperative effort ushered in an era of growth, organized efficiency, and far-spreading evangelical activity. These developments made possible the evangelization of America by Protestants. Denominations had never cooperated before in this way, and certainly never have since. The lack of rivalry and competition, and the scale on which the Sunday School evangelization was conducted, shook the entire country.

During the period from 1825 to near the end of the century, the emphasis of United States Sunday Schools was on basics. First, the leaders wanted children to accept Christ. And second, they wanted to impart Bible knowledge. This is important to remember. During the rapid expansion of Sunday Schools, the emphasis was on salvation and Bible content, resulting in increased knowledge and changed lives.

Three Emphases

Early leaders in the American Sunday School Union carefully evaluated what was happening in Sunday Schools. This enabled them to determine what should be done to help produce more effective Sunday Schools, and thereby more effective ministry to the young people in this country. The leaders determined that in order to help Sunday Schools grow, there were three areas they ought to emphasize. They concluded that the first area was improvement in the quality of education. The second emphasis was on organization. And the third was on the extension of the Sunday School to areas that hadn't yet been reached. Let's consider each of these in order.

1. Quality of education. Sunday School originally was designed to educate young people. Since Christianity thrives with an educated constituency, when the church is untrained, it is weak. Eavey observed that through the centuries when the church gave attention to teaching the Word, the result was substantial progress in helping individual Christians to mature. And likewise, where education was neglected, the church became weak and ineffective. Sunday School was designed as a means to teach the Word of God effectively.

John Owen, the Puritan scholar, wrote, "More knowledge is ordinarily diffused, especially among the young and ignorant, by an hour's catechetical exercise than by many hours' continual discourse" (Eavey, *Christian Education,* p. 221). This meant that one hour of teaching, including discussion, could accomplish far more than many hours of preaching. And this observation came from a scholar/preacher.

The original intent of the catechism was to stimulate discussion. It is unfortunate that studying the catechism deteriorated into rote question/answer methodology. Church leaders for centuries have known of the need for effective teaching. Concern about teaching methods is not new in our generation. More than 100 years ago, the American Sunday School Union emphasized the use of methodology that would make the educational process as effective as possible.

In order to accomplish this, Union leaders examined the curriculum employed in teaching. By the 1820s, they recommended taking a biblical text of 10 to 20 verses for study. They attempted to discover appropriate texts for any given age, so that they could select "lessons" for teaching.

In the mid 1800s many denominations produced their own lessons. The great confusion that this caused finally led to the creation of a "Uniform Lesson Committee" in 1872. The Union asked this committee to select appropriate passages for particular age groups, so that all Sunday Schools could follow a similar pattern.

The most important aspect of curriculum development was the continuing emphasis on "the Bible as textbook." The purpose always was to instruct pupils in the facts of the Bible. The lessons challenged teachers to apply the truths within the Bible content. Although the emphasis on memorization moderated during this period, programs of Bible memorization continued to play a significant role in Sunday Schools.

The educational success of the Sunday School instruction presented the leaders with a problem. As children learned to read, they hungered for more literature. But in the regions where there were pioneer Sunday Schools, rarely was there any literature to read. So the American Sunday School Union wrote and produced literature and emphasized the library as an integral part of organizing a Sunday School.

By 1830 the Union had produced more the 200 different titles. In 1845 they began offering libraries of 100 bound volumes for 10 dollars. Stephen Paxson and others encouraged local residents to contribute at least half of this amount. Three other sets of volumes followed this first one. Since in many frontier communities the Sunday School library was the only reading material in town, those volumes received great attention.

The Union produced other literature to help improve the quality of education. Union leaders circulated instructions to pastors suggesting how they could strengthen the Sunday Schools in their churches. The Union stressed the primary position of the pastor, and emphasized that an effective Sunday School would help him accomplish his task.

The Sunday School Union published other books for superintendents and for teachers, spelling out in great detail the responsibilities, and recommended methods to fulfill them. One volume went into great detail describing the qualities of both the good and the bad teacher. This small volume titled *Sunday School Phenomena,* published in 1852, contained chapters on "The Indifferent Pastor,"

"The Incompetent Superintendent," and "The Careless Teacher" (American Sunday School Union, p. 44).

There was a strong attempt to make leaders aware of the responsibility of Sunday School teaching. In *Sunday School Phenomena,* the incompetent superintendent was described as one who infects his teachers so that, "They become blind to each other's errors and deficiencies and pass on, mutually satisfied, while a hundred or two of precious children are hastening to the judgment of the great day, impenitent and unforgiven" *(Ibid.,* p. 57).

2. Organization. While leaders of the Sunday School Union were concerned about education, they also had a second major concern during this period. They felt that the Sunday School movement needed greater organization. As the number of schools grew, the problems of coordination grew also. Denominational involvement in Sunday School further complicated the situation. Each group wanted to emphasize its own distinctives.

It is surprising that the denominations allowed the Union, as the coordinating agency, so much influence. Even as individual denominational programs grew, the American Sunday School Union's coordination and unification of all evangelical teachers in their common concern was encouraged. Their bond was the centrality of Jesus Christ, with a common emphasis on teaching the Word of God. With agreement on these crucial concepts, minor differences were easily resolved.

One of the early organizational efforts stressed the Sunday School convention. The first convention was held in New York in 1832, and the second in Philadelphia a year later. These were designed to challenge teachers and superintendents, and to encourage them to see a vision of their high and noble calling. Although enthusiasm for conventions fluctuated, their popularity generally increased throughout the century.

In the rural areas the convention idea became very strong. Since many Sunday School teachers were serving God in isolation, the convention often was their only encouragement. In 1865 Stephen Paxson presented a plan to the Seventh Annual Sunday School Convention of Illinois. He proposed to organize the entire state with individual county and even township conventions. The motion was seconded by Dwight L. Moody, and 2,500 dollars was raised to support the plan. Paxson got busy and didn't rest until the entire 102 counties, and many townships too, were organized.

By 1860, with more than three million Sunday School students, it was becoming increasingly obvious that with the growth and diversity of Sunday Schools, the American Sunday School Union had too great a task. And so it relinquished regional coordination to the conventions, and the Union worked with the leaders of these local, state, and international conventions.

Another effective approach to organization that relieved the Union leaders from their high level of responsibility involved mobilizing local pastors. It was rightly concluded that if pastors could be encouraged to take the responsibility for overseeing the Sunday Schools, such supervision could be done far more effectively. In one Union volume this viewpoint was stated strongly. "There would be no extravagance in saying that the strength and efficiency of our Sunday Schools would be *quadrupled at once* by the earnest and hearty countenance and cooperation of the ministry and these other influences that would be sure to follow" *(Ibid.,* p. 36).

In the late 1800s a well-known pastor, Dr. Asa Bullard, described another pastor whose church had a membership of 536, with 512 attending the Sunday School. "The minister in charge of this church would visit one of his members who absented himself from Sunday School, to plead with him against this dereliction of duty, as if he had given up family worship" (Trumbull, *Yale Lectures,* p. 195).

But in stressing organization to the pastors, the teachers were not neglected. Union leaders wrote that they hoped all teachers would regularly attend the preaching services. This was one way that teachers would communicate the importance of worship to the children whom they were teaching. The Union recognized that when teachers and pastors supported each other, the ministry of each was strengthened.

However, even at this late date, the Union recognized that some pastors saw the Sunday Schools as a "clumsy appendage," rather than a "beautiful and powerful machine." When this was the case, the subsequent rivalry and conflict led to a weakening and disorganization, rather than to a smoothly coordinated effort.

3. Extension. In addition to the emphasis in the 1800s on education and organization, the third, and perhaps most important emphasis of the American Sunday School Union, was extension. The Union made sure that Sunday Schools followed the people west, and ministered to them all along the way. It was a period of missionary outreach, and men like Stephen Paxson enabled such growth to occur. Indeed, they brought it about.

By 1830 the desire to extend the ministry of Sunday School into newly developed regions was strong. The pioneers were isolated, and rarely had churches or schools. Education usually was nonexistent and consisted only of what the parents could provide for their children. Since most parents were poorly educated, and had little spiritual preparation, children rarely received formal or biblical education.

In an 1830 Union meeting, 2,000 participants unanimously passed a resolution to establish "Sabbath Schools" in every town in the Mississippi Valley. This was an area of 1.3 million square miles where four million people lived, one tenth of whom were children. This area extended from the Allegheny mountains to the Rockies, and from Michigan to Louisiana.

The experiences of Stephen Paxson were common to those missionaries serving in this region. With little money, they suffered great hardships to extend the Sunday School. Even when local individuals were helpful, there were problems. One night Paxson had been given lodging by a settler. Paxson's daughter wrote of her father, "He was six feet tall; the cot given to him to sleep upon was short. . . . He forgot the limitation of his cot, and as he fell asleep, extended himself his full length. His feet, covered by a white sheet went right through an open space between the logs in the wall of the house where the mud filling had dropped out. He was awakened early in the morning by the fierce barking of a dog and the cry of a boy: 'Mr. Missionary! Mr. Missionary! Wake up and take in your feet or Jowler will bite your toes off!'" (Drury, *A Fruitful Life,* p. 195)

In order to finance these Mississippi Valley endeavors, concerned Christians contributed many thousands of dollars at meetings held in Boston, New York, Philadelphia, and Charleston. But the greatest of these meetings was held in Washington, D.C. Many senators and congressmen attended, including Daniel Webster and Francis Scott Key. A Washington newspaper described the meeting as "one of the most important ever held in this country."

Growing out of this major campaign, almost 100 missionaries established Sunday Schools in about half of the ten thousand settlements in the Mississippi Valley. Each school that raised at least five dollars received a library worth ten dollars. More than one million volumes were distributed this way. The impact of this distribution upon the educational and literary growth of this region was incalculable.

The Union inaugurated a similar project in the South. While the land area was smaller, the population was more dense. Of the 800,000 children in the region, 300,000 were black. Most of the families in the South were quite poor and the children received little spiritual or general education. Since there was great civil conflict during most of this time, the campaign was limited.

The campaign made significant contributions, however. Many Sunday Schools were started and churches strengthened. Bible study increased, and general education received great encouragement. One thousand libraries of 120 bound volumes each were prepared and contributed to the public schools of the south. C.B. Eavey wrote that the Southern campaign did much to encourage the youth of the South to seek education. He wrote that the spiritual impact was great, and in addition to the spiritual influence, free public education was encouraged very much (Eavey, *Christian Education*, p. 250)

Because of the great drive to establish Sunday Schools in the Midwest and South, by about the turn of the century, the total Sunday School scholars in this country almost equaled all of the Sunday School scholars in the rest of the world. In the United States there were about eight million students in Sunday Schools, with one million teachers.

When Clarence Benson wrote a history of Christian education, he listed several results of the Mississippi Valley and Southern Campaigns. Hundreds of thousands of children and adults came to Christ. Thousands of churches were started. In one 15-year period, 4 out of 5 churches established in the Mississippi Valley grew out of Sunday Schools. Entire communities received religious instruction, and were stimulated to seek other education. General education was promoted by the libraries that were provided, and Sunday School leaders spearheaded the drive for legislation that would establish free public schools.

Impact of the Sunday School

We cannot comprehend the impact that Sunday School had upon the United States during this period. H.C. Trumbull wrote that in the latter part of the 1700s, Bible study, Bible teaching, the church, and spiritual vitality were at a low ebb. However, by the latter 1800s, spiritual vitality growing out of effective Bible teaching and study reached a high point. This was due to the powerful impact of the Sunday School. It was God's tool to evangelize the nation and to energize the church *(Yale Lectures,* p. 142).

One young collegian living in the late 1800s described the importance of Sunday School to him, even though the class often disagreed on the interpretation of some biblical passages. "There was no lecturing, no exhorting and little agreement. Whatever the day's passage and title might be, that hour woke us up for the week and sent us out to take our lives more seriously. It also broadened and freshened our Bible concepts in a notable degree" (Fergusson, *Historic Chapters,* p. 130).

In 1888, H. Clay Trumbull related an account of the place and importance of Sunday School. He shared the testimony of the well-known religious educator, Horace Bushnell, a teacher of Trumbull's who had tried to get Trumbull to forsake Sunday School and turn to the pastorate. Near the end of his life, Bushnell said, "Trumbull, you knew better than I did where the Lord wanted you. I honestly thought the pulpit was a bigger place for you, and I tried to get you into it. But now I've come to see that the work you are in is the greatest work in the world." After a brief pause he continued, "Sometimes I think it's the *only* work there is in the world" (Trumbull, *Yale Lectures,* p. vii).

7
The Fall and Rise
of the Sunday School

As America celebrated its 100th anniversary, the strength of the U.S. Sunday School was recognized around the world. Emile de Laveleye, a professor from the University of Liege, Belgium wrote in 1876, "The Sunday School is one of the strongest foundations of the republican institutions of the United States" (Trumbull, *Yale Lectures,* p. 133) A few years later, Trumbull wrote that "America has been practically saved to Christianity and the religion of the Bible by the Sunday School. . . . The new agency practically stayed the progress of error and unbelief, and rescued the children alike of those who had lapsed from the faith, and those who never had the faith" *(Ibid.,* p. 122).

Lloyd George, prime minister of Great Britain early in the 1900s testified, "Personally, I know what a Sunday School can do. All the best training I ever had was in a Sunday School. It has become the university of the people for the study of the higher and deeper knowledge of religion."

And yet with such accolades ringing loud and clear, the Sunday School went into decline. After almost a century and a half of dynamic, incredible growth, the statistics showed that 1916 was a year of loss. And it wasn't an isolated year. Nationally, the direction of Sunday School went downward in the following years, even to the present time.

It is difficult to understand how a vital, growing institution in the late 1800s could become a shadow of its former glory, in just a few years. At the end of the 1800s, the Sunday School's emphasis was on growth and outreach. Trumbull asserted that it was never satisfactory to have in the Sunday School only those children whose parents came to church. The Sunday School should be reaching out as long as there were any persons to reach.

Trumbull's account of one superintendent accurately depicts the attitude of the day. He related that whenever this superintendent saw a man who should attend Sunday School, he invited him to come. But in addition to that, he asked the man's wife to encourage him to attend. He then asked the man's children to invite their father to attend. He also encouraged members of the class to invite the man to attend. The pastor was asked to encourage the man to attend. And then the superintendent would look for another person to recruit in the same way. His attitude was one of excitement and enthusiasm. He knew that Sunday School was valuable, and he wanted others to benefit.

In major cities, Sunday Schools were used as evangelistic tools. For example, in Philadelphia several young laymen went into the back streets of the city and gathered together a small group of Sunday School students—only about 30 at first. But as those laymen worked and ministered, their little group grew. Their work and the work of those who attended began to show fruit. From this small group of 30, a Sunday School of more than 2,000 resulted and eventually, a new church was founded, which in turn generated the founding of other churches.

By this time, Sunday School was not only for children. In 1886 the Presbyterian General Assembly supported the concept of a whole church Sunday School. The General Assembly declared, "It is exceedingly desirable that the entire congregation, old and young, be permanently connected with the Sunday School, either as scholars or teachers" (*Ibid.,* p. 192). Dr. Archibald Alexander of Princeton supported the same idea, emphasizing that all should participate, whether as teachers or students, sometimes as one and sometimes as the other.

The Sunday School movement became so successful that the demand for Bibles and other Christian literature far exceeded the available supply. Bible societies and tract societies were founded to provide the literature needed. Other organizations were established to provide supplies and information for Sunday School workers and students.

But then, the Sunday School declined. Although seemingly strong and influential, it began losing vitality and influence. And within a half century, one writer for *Life* magazine had marshalled enough evidence to refer to Sunday School as "the most wasted hour of the week." In those 50 years the total number of persons enrolled in Sunday School increased significantly, but the percentage of population attending declined. Even worse, many felt that the spiritual impact for those in attendance was far weaker than it had been previously, because there was less emphasis on Bible instruction.

Reasons for Decline

A brief review of the trends in Sunday School during the period from 1875 to the present may help us to understand what happened, and why.

As the Sunday School movement gained momentum, the American Sunday School Union leaders soon saw that they could not control and coordinate the entire Sunday School movement. They determined that it was better to relinquish control to the conventions that had already been providing some coordination.

In 1832 the first National Sunday School Convention was held. Its purpose was to challenge and motivate, as well as to determine policy on issues that affected the entire Sunday School movement. In 1875 the first International Sunday School Convention was held in Baltimore. At this convention Canada participated, thus making the convention international.

1. Emphasis on organization. Between 1875 and 1905, 11 international conventions were held. One of the purposes of the conventions was to organize and systematize the ministry of Sunday School. The conventions raised money and made decisions about the world outreach of Sunday School. But another purpose was to help the individual teacher. E. Morris Fergusson wrote, "To attend a convention revealed to the local worker his chosen cause operating on a wider field, broadened his fellowship, inspired him to new effort, and returned him with loyalty to church and denomination intelligently reinforced" *(Historic Chapters,* p. 30).

And yet the emphasis on organization seems to be one of the factors contributing to the lessened influence of Sunday School. The International Sunday School Association was formed at the World Sunday School Convention in Rome in 1907. Some felt that to leave the work of Sunday School direction to the somewhat haphazard efforts of a triennial convention was unwise. While the formation of the International Sunday School Association was a step forward for organization, it would prove to be a giant step backward for the Sunday School.

In spite of apparent success in organization, the Sunday School was not strengthened. In fact, it seemed to grow weaker. C.B. Eavey suggested a major factor in the cause of this decline. He wrote in his *History of Christian Education,* "The Sunday School was Protestantism's most important single agency for doing the work of God in the world. It is pertinent, therefore, to ask why it underwent decline after 1916. This question has its basic answer in the fact that leadership became liberal in theology" (p. 266). But this decline did not happen instantaneously. It happened as there came a shift in leadership emphasis, through attempts at organizing the Sunday School movement.

One of the key characteristics of the convention system was the shared decision-making. Those who were deeply involved in the work of Sunday School around the world determined policy and direction through their votes. Laymen were Sunday School leaders as well as policy makers.

When the International Sunday School Association was created in 1907, a new constitution was proposed and adopted by the World Sunday School Convention. That constitution specified that full decision-making power would be in the hands of the Executive Committee which actually was the corporation. By this one decision, the World Sunday School Convention took the guidance of the Sunday School movement from the hands of laymen and assigned it to professionals.

At the same time mainline denominations were increasingly dissatisfied with the direction of Sunday School. They wanted more control over curriculum and organization. So in 1910 the Sunday School Council of Evangelical Denominations was formed. Many of the denominational representatives were growing more liberal in theology, and all were professional leaders, not laymen.

These denominational leaders, along with leaders in higher education, were strongly influenced by an organization that had been established in 1903, the Religious Education Association. This liberal association equated religious education (which included non-Christian religions) with Christian education. From its inception, the organization had a strong impact on the directions of religious education in this country.

Since the International Sunday School Association and the Sunday School Council of Evangelical Denominations faced a potential conflict over their interest in directing the Sunday School movement, it was appropriate that they should consolidate their efforts. This they did in 1922, and became the International Council of Religious Education.

The direction for Sunday School that was set during the early 1900s had a great influence on the later course of the Sunday School movement. One of the important elements in that direction was the professionalism that entered the movement. Instead of being controlled and directed by laymen, the denominational leaders and professional religious educators controlled the direction of Sunday Schools.

2. *Experience-centered curriculum.* But that by itself was not the most significant reason. Even more significant was that this allowed a second change in direction to take place. The second change involved the curriculum that was provided for Sunday Schools. Although the curriculum during most of the 1800s had been of mixed quality, it had one key characteristic. It stressed learning the facts of the Bible. In the better schools these facts were then applied to life.

Under the influence of professionals, there was a strong desire to increase the standardization that already had begun. The International Council of Religious Education promoted a curriculum with a "Life-centered Philosophy." Under the Council, the starting point of curriculum changed. In previous attempts to improve and systematize curriculum, the Bible always had been the starting point, with an attempt to teach students the content of the Word of God. The aim was primarily an intellectual one. Students learned Bible facts.

When the emphasis shifted, the experience of the student became the starting point. Instead of teaching the Bible because it was important to know biblical truths, the curriculum began with the problems of the pupil and sought to help the pupil find the answers to those problems. The emphasis was on Christian living, with Christian education and character education becoming synonymous.

It is educationally sound to begin with the needs of the pupil. However, the theological perspective of those involved in curriculum reform was liberal, not conservative. This meant that the Bible was ascribed little more value than other literature that might be used. Subsequently, the curriculum increasingly turned from the study of the Bible to other sources. As a result, students failed to learn the Bible.

One positive consequence of the educational emphasis was the trend toward graded curriculum materials which were educationally far superior to the old materials. And yet the actual gain in Bible knowledge decreased, due to the shift from Bible content to experience-centered curriculum.

During this period, the old uniform lessons were looked upon with great disfavor, and by about 1930 most of the denominations had developed their own graded curriculum materials. However, most of the mainline denominations also provided high-experience, low-Bible-content curriculum similar to the International Council of Religious Education curriculum.

While other factors contributed to weakening U.S. Sunday Schools, these seem to be the two most important elements: Laymen lost control and direction of the Sunday School movement, and the curriculum failed to emphasize regular and intensive study of the content of the Bible. Both lay direction and Bible instruction were basic to the early Sunday School movement. When these elements were removed, the Sunday School movement declined.

Growth in Some Areas

However, the picture of Sunday Schools should not be viewed quite so bleakly, for all Sunday Schools did not decline. Those Sunday Schools that had leaders who were theologically conservative continued to see growth and blessing. The denominations that remained conservative, such as the Southern Baptists, saw phenomenal growth early in this century. Smaller denominations, such as the Assemblies of God and others, continued to show gains in Sunday School. Those denominations operated apart from the International Council of Religious Education.

In recent years Sunday Schools have played a vital role in some of America's churches, those of conservative or fundamental denominations, and also independent or denominational churches which are conservative theologically. The Bible Baptist Fellowship, an association of fundamentalist Bible churches, has reported extremely large Sunday School ministries. Other conservative churches, both denominational and independent, have likewise demonstrated the continued effectiveness of Sunday Schools.

One factor that has contributed to the continued success of conservative Sunday School ministries has been the curriculum materials produced by independent publishers. When the majority of denominational curriculum offerings were liberal, these independent publishers provided a biblical alternative that enabled Sunday Schools to flourish.

David C. Cook

One of the earliest independent publishers of Sunday School curriculum materials was David C. Cook. Cook's father was in the printing business, so David had an understanding of the technical aspects of printing. But instead of joining his father in business, Cook founded a company of his own to distribute sewing machine accessories.

Although Cook developed quite a successful business headquartered in downtown Chicago, he soon found his attention drawn away from his sewing machine accessory business, and toward his real love, Sunday School ministry. While teaching Sunday School as a layman, Cook recognized the need for high quality, attractive curriculum materials. While some biblical materials were available, most were drab and uninviting.

Finally, Cook felt so compelled to focus his energies on Sunday School that he sold his small business to his partner, George Bent, so that he could produce and publish curriculum materials full-time. The same energy that originally he had devoted to the sewing machine business was redirected to printing and publishing.

The first material published by the David C. Cook Publishing Company in 1875 was *Our Sunday School Quarterly,* followed by a Sunday School paper, *Our Sunday School Gem.* The materials were fresh and bright, and received immediate acceptance. Soon, Cook produced other materials needed for instructing and promoting Sunday Schools.

An innovative feature of the Cook curriculum materials was the graded aspect. One passage of Scripture was chosen for study each Sunday. But rather than have all age-levels study the biblical passage in the same way, it was handled differently for each age-group. This meant that the basic emphasis for all classes was similar, but the outline, methods and illustrations were graded to the specific age-group being taught.

As the Cook Publishing Company grew and expanded, other products were added. Yet, Sunday School curriculum materials and literature were always the main emphasis. Sunday School curriculum in the tradition of the founder continues to be the emphasis of the David C. Cook Publishing Company.

Clarence H. Benson

Some years after Cook started his company, another man from Chicago had a similar vision, but for a different reason. Clarence H. Benson, in charge of Christian Education at the Moody Bible Institute, grew increasingly concerned about the need for high quality Sunday School curriculum materials that were strong in Bible content. While there were many resources available, there was no curriculum that systematically covered the entire Bible. Graded lessons from the denominations and the International Council of Religious Education were biblically weak. The old uniform lessons were woefully inadequate and dealt with the Bible in the pick-and-choose method, not systematically.

So Benson mobilized his students in a curriculum writing course at the Moody Bible Institute. During the latter part of the 1920s and the early 1930s, they wrote the All-Bible Graded Series. Two of the students in that curriculum course were sisters, Lois and Mary LeBar, who were to become highly influential Christian educators, known and respected around the world. Benson had determined that this course was to be comprehensive, consecutive, and complete. But Benson was an educator and a scholar, not a publisher or a businessman. So he enlisted the help of a friend, Victor E. Cory, to assist in the production and distribution of the curriculum materials developed at the Institute.

Victor E. Cory

Cory originally worked as an engineer with the Commonwealth Edison Electric Company in Chicago, but he felt God's direction to move into management in a Christian organization. So he accepted a management position at the Tabernacle Publishing Company and later became assistant manager at Moody Press, where he met Clarence Benson.

Victor Cory agreed to publish the curriculum materials written by Benson and his students if someone would lend him the money for the project. When William R. Thomas of Chicago agreed, the foundation was laid for Scripture Press Publications. In the early years of Scripture Press, Victor and Bernice Cory provided most of the company's manpower. The early lessons, edited by Bernice and printed under the direction of Victor, were put together on the Corys' kitchen table in Chicago. As the company grew, and the demand increased, larger facilities were secured, until Scripture Press Publications relocated in Wheaton, Illinois. Later, Scripture Press added offices in other states and incorporated in Canada and England.

When the assets of Scripture Press Publications increased significantly, the Corys, rather than maintaining the company as a personal asset, established Scripture Press Foundation and assigned all of the assets to it. Scripture Press Foundation later became Scripture Press Ministries, and continues as a not-for-profit ministry organization to insure the fulfillment of the Corys' vision through Scripture Press.

The essential elements that were written into the All-Bible Graded Series have continued through revision and updating. Benson and his students incorporated the following guidelines into the series:

1. The Bible and the Bible alone is the basis of true religion.
2. All Scripture is profitable for instruction.
3. The lesson should be adapted to the capacity of the pupil.

4. Bible instruction can be made personal and practical.
5. Bible instruction should parallel the Christian year.
6. Repetition should not impede progress or lesson interest (Benson, *A Popular History,* pp. 229-233).

Henrietta Mears

At about the same time Scripture Press Publications was beginning, a Christian educator on the West Coast became involved in a similar endeavor. Henrietta Mears, director of Christian education at the First Presbyterian Church of Hollywood, California, felt the same need for high-quality, biblical curriculum materials. So she began writing them.

The materials that Miss Mears produced followed the educational philosophy that she held dear. She believed that "Christian education recognizes the inspired Word of God, not only as its text and the sum of its message, but also as the source of the principles by which successful Christian education may be carried on" (Ethel May Baldwin and David V. Benson, *Henrietta Mears and How She Did It,* Regal, 1966, p. 56). She had a deep and continuing loyalty to the authoritative Word of God, and she desired Bible-based curriculum materials that were attractive and educationally sound. This desire thrust her into curriculum design and production.

As Miss Mears began examining the materials available to her teachers at First Presbyterian Church, she was appalled. She saw one Primary lesson titled, "Amos Denounces Self-Indulgence." In a Junior lesson she read with great horror, "Paul survived his shipwreck because he had eaten his carrots and was strong" *(Ibid.,* pp. 60-61). She rejected the common approach of many writers who skip back and forth across the centuries of Bible history in their lessons, calling it the "Grasshopper Method." She preferred a chronological approach that was graded to a pupil's school grade and she demanded that the material be attractive.

Miss Mears and her associates wrote lesson after lesson. In order to make the spartan materials more attractive, they cut out pictures from old calendars and other sources and pasted them onto the lesson materials. Soon, others began hearing of the success of her materials and wanted to use them. As the demand grew, associates and acquaintances joined in the ministry, supplying creative, technical, and production assistance. Within 12 years after joining the staff of the First Presbyterian Church, Miss Mears led Gospel Light Press to become one of the larger independent publishers of Sunday School literature in the United States.

Originally, Sunday School leaders hoped that there would be coordination of the regional Sunday School Associations through a national or international convention. While this did not happen, the evangelical churches and workers who continued conducting regional conventions received great help from the publishers of Christian education curriculum materials. David C. Cook, Gospel Light, and Scripture Press, along with other publishers, have invested great sums of money to help underwrite speakers, workshop leaders, and other services needed for successful conventions. Across the country today, many conventions and associations exist because of the substantial financial support provided by the publishing houses and other parachurch agencies. Many feel that this support, in large part, is responsible for the quality of Christian education today.

National Sunday School Association

In 1945 the National Sunday School Association was organized under the auspices of the National Association of Evangelicals. The National Sunday School Association continued for 25 years and assisted in coordinating Sunday School and Christian education endeavors. Today, the regional associations continue to minister to professionals and laymen alike, through conventions and other Christian education activities.

The present health of the evangelical Sunday School and other Christian education ministries is a tribute to the involvement of lay persons. Because they are the heart of the Sunday School movement, lay persons will still determine the future of Sunday School. It is only through a vast force of Christians mobilized to serve God that we *will* *see* the success that we *must see*. The remaining chapters of this book are dedicated to the concept that we *can* mobilize this force. We *must* mobilize this force.

8
Sunday School
and the Church
of the 1980s

In the 200 years between Robert Raikes and the present, Sunday Schools have grown, changed, and made an impact on the world. The development of the United States, and many other nations, has been influenced dramatically by the Sunday School movement. People have been converted to Christ and have matured through the influence of Sunday Schools. In addition to the spiritual values, secular society has benefited as Sunday Schools have stimulated interest in general education.

Yet some maintain that Sunday Schools are outdated and hopelessly ineffective. Others have suggested "operating" on the Sunday School, with suggestions ranging from cosmetic surgery to total removal. We hear terms of derision such as "like a Sunday School class," or "as exciting as a Sunday School picnic," to describe boring, irrelevant activities.

But we *have* Sunday Schools today. There are very few churches that don't conduct either a Sunday School or a program that is its first cousin. Even the detractors of Sunday School rarely recommend total removal; they usually want to "tinker" with the program. Most recommendations focus on superficial issues—using facilities other than the church building, meeting at a different time of the day or the week, or using different methods or a new format. They recognize that the concept of Sunday School is a good one, but the program could be improved greatly by certain modifications.

Sunday School Reflects the Church

And yet Sunday Schools are an integral part of most church programs. With all of their problems, Sunday Schools continue as a significant ministry. Sunday Schools are much like our own children in that we love them deeply, but often are more aware of their weaknesses and shortcomings than anyone else is. We often feel frustrated with our children because they reflect our own weaknesses and inadequacies. So we find it easy to criticize and condemn them for making us see those characteristics that we dislike most in ourselves.

In the same way, Sunday Schools reflect the strengths and the weaknesses of our churches. Dr. Gene Getz, founder and pastor of Fellowship Bible Church in Dallas, Texas said, "Sunday School structures usually also reflect the overall emphasis of the church. If it's Bible teaching, so goes the Sunday School. If it's relationships, so goes the Sunday School. The strengths and weaknesses of the Sunday School are the strengths and weaknesses of the church" (National Christian Education Study Seminar Report, *The Sunday School Today and Tomorrow,* Scripture Press Ministries, 1975, p. 33).

But we often fail to perceive the reality of this profound observation by Dr. Getz. We can easily condemn the Sunday School for its faults and weaknesses. But even as we are criticizing this arm of the church, we need to see that such an indictment should be made of the entire church, rather than singling out one particular program.

Occasionally focusing on one ministry of the church, and recognizing its weaknesses and strengths produces benefits. Through such a study, leaders of a church often see that the strengths and weaknesses apply to more programs than just the Sunday School. Leaders who find that teachers have little enthusiasm for their Sunday School ministry may realize that the overall church ministry is characterized by apathy and low commitment. A church with a core of enthusiastic but superficial teachers may recognize that their Sunday School is part of a church with great excitement but with little spiritual maturity.

This inseparable relationship between the strengths and weaknesses of the Sunday School and the church demonstrates the substantial strength of the Sunday School in the United States. Such identification between church and Sunday School did not occur in all countries, and the ministry of Sunday School has been weaker in those places.

Three Sunday School Types

As we keep in mind the principle that Sunday School often reflects an image of the total church, there are at least three distinct types of Sunday Schools existing at the present time. These are the traditional Sunday Schools, the evangelistic Sunday Schools, and the educational/fellowship Sunday Schools. Even as we consider these types, we must realize that many variations are possible. Most Sunday Schools tend toward one of these categories, but few are exclusively one or the other.

1. Traditional Sunday Schools. A Traditional Sunday School is one that is continuing primarily because there was a Sunday School in the past. Teachers often serve out of guilt or obligation, instead of deep commitment to a vital, ongoing ministry. Such a Sunday School may be characterized by some children, very few teens, no single adults, and few, if any, married couples. Or, it may have many in attendance, participating in the routine out of guilt or obligation. This type of Sunday School follows the *form* of the program, but denies the *power* that used to characterize such a ministry.

These are the schools that James D. Murch described in *Teach or Perish.* "The average schools are plodding along on a treadmill of worn-out tradition and mediocrity, quite unaware of their responsibility to a changing world and of their potentiality in bringing in a new and better day. They go along doing the things they have always done, keeping the organizational wheels greased and turning, teaching hit-skip portions of the Bible in a seven year curricular merry-go-round" (Eerdmans, 1961, p. 73). Baptist clergyman Wesley Shrader writing for *Life* magazine in 1958 quoted a boy attending a Sunday School. He said, "I've had enough. I'll never go to Sunday School again. It's the most wasted hour of the week" (11 February 1958, p. 100). Someone else heard a youngster simply state, "Sunday School stinks!"

Those of us who are evangelical like to accuse the liberal churches of such a condition. And indeed, such is the emphasis of many liberal churches. C.B. Eavey claimed that when the priority of the Bible was replaced with a man-oriented emphasis, Sunday School declined. Churches and individuals lost their enthusiasm.

And yet evangelical churches often conduct this type of traditional Sunday School. A sterile orthodoxy can generate an apathetic response in the same way that liberal theology does. Eavey observed that some evangelicals contributed to the decline that is evident in Traditional Sunday Schools. Those were the leaders who refused to forsake old ways or to adopt anything new in methods or materials. They kept on because they had always done it that way (Eavey, *Christian Education,* p. 268). Murch characterized this kind of Sunday School as having a "deadly conformity to traditional routines and a lamentable apathy concerning educational advance. There is no vision of enlargement adequate to the needs of the times" *(Teach or Perish,* p. 52).

Any time a group of individuals carries on a program simply because there was one in the past, they may produce deadly apathy. Each generation must rediscover the purpose and meaning of its activities. If careful attention is not given to the reason for a particular program and the benefits resulting from it, a lifeless traditionalism can easily set in. Some have called it "institutional rigor mortis," others, "hardening of the categories." Whatever the term, the Traditional Sunday School has passed the status of retreat, and more often seems to be in total rout.

Because this type of Sunday School probably reflects its church's overall attitude, what can be the solution for those involved in the program? A remedy must include a rediscovery of purpose, not just for the Sunday School, but for the entire ministry of the church. Ideally, the recognized leaders of the church should take the lead in such an evaluation. But if they don't, others in the church can begin the examination.

If an individual Sunday School teacher evaluates his class, he can discover the potential for a ministry that coincides with the historical purpose and emphasis of the Church, the body of Chirst. As he becomes infectiously enthusiastic about such a discovery, he will begin to see lives transformed. Then he can encourage other teachers to do the same sort of evaluation. And when they see transformations, others will take notice. Often, an entire church has regained a sense of biblical purpose and dynamic, from the work of one person who teaches the Bible and gains a vision of what God wants for that ministry.

The lessons from the history of the Sunday School movement teach us that one person can have a dramatic impact. Individual commitment to purpose is contagious. The Holy Spirit often chooses to work through the efforts of one person sold out to God, and many times that one person has been a layman. Whether a Robert Raikes, a William Fox, or a Stephen Paxson, God has blessed the ministry of laymen.

2. Evangelistic Sunday Schools. The second type of Sunday School that is quite prevalent today is the Evangelistic Sunday School. Many of the features that characterize the Traditional Sunday School are reversed in the Evangelistic Sunday School. There is an excitement and a vitality. Things are happening, and people are enthusiastic about the anticipated results. High visibility in the community often characterizes this type of school.

This Sunday School does not exist in isolation, but is part of the overall program of the church, and reflects the philosophy of the leaders. Words such as *aggressive, promotional, active,* and *visible* describe most programs in this type of church, and particularly, the Sunday School ministry. Since the emphasis is on expansion and reaching out, these churches concentrate on those who are not regular attenders.

Often, the Evangelistic Sunday School operates a fleet of buses to transport the large number of students recruited. It is unfortunate that many people, including some participating in the program, feel that the buses are the heart of the program. They are not. They are a means to accomplish the specific goals that have been set. The Evangelistic Sunday School can operate with or without buses. Although buses are an asset, the ministry is far more than machinery.

Being merely a method, busing is subject to modification and change. One pastor said that the key to success in his ministry was buses. Such a view is terribly nearsighted and elevates a method above the true goals of the program. For the key to the success of the Evangelistic Sunday School is far more than method. It is vision and commitment to evangelism and expansion. Substituting the goal of running a fleet of buses for the goal of reaching the unchurched dooms the ministry, just as surely as liberal theology does.

Many have accused the Evangelistic Sunday School of sensationalism and preoccupation with numbers. And yet if the goal of the program is to reach the unchurched, every person who participates represents the achievement of that goal. And that goal is valid. As we will consider in the next chapter, a major part of the Great Commission to "make disciples of all the nations," is evangelism. We cannot make disciples until persons choose to follow Christ. The goal of reaching the unreached, giving them the opportunity to follow Christ, is a biblical goal.

One woman testified to the importance of the ministry of an Evangelistic Sunday School. She was divorced, with four children, little income, and even less spiritual resource. She felt very alone and miserable, and related how, "the Lord and I weren't on speaking terms then." She told how three of her children attended Sunday School the first week of the Sunday School bus run. A few weeks later the fourth child went. Finally, she began attending.

Before long she and her two oldest sons accepted Christ. Soon after, the other two children followed their example. She credits her salvation and the subsequent transformation of her family to the outreach of that Sunday School through a bus ministry *(Baptist Leader,* August 1979, p. 5).

This story could be repeated countless times, for the Evangelistic Sunday School reaches those who have need but little contact with God's Word. However, it is important to realize that gathering in the students on a Sunday is only one part of the outreach. Personal contact through the week with those who attend is the heart of an outreach program. It includes visiting the parents of the children who attend. It means finding out the needs of a family and being available for God to use in helping to meet those needs. Church members participate in all aspects of the ministry such as contacting and inviting students, instructing them on Sunday morning, and visiting through the week in a follow-up ministry on a personal level.

The Evangelistic Sunday School reflects the fervor of many of the early Sunday Schools in this country, for it seeks to minister to those who are unchurched. It often reaches children whose parents are unconcerned, and then moves right into the home to minister to those parents who would never take the initiative. This significant ministry offers church members a place of service, and gives the church high visibility in the community, because the church is reaching out rather than withdrawing.

But the Evangelistic Sunday School is not without problems. Bringing in large numbers of unchurched children and adults creates unique situations. Most churches minister to those who are familiar with church routine, and comfortable in the classroom-sanctuary context. But this is not the situation when the unchurched are brought in. So they must be carefully ministered to if they are to benefit from the experience. Teachers need special preparation, above and beyond that required in a more traditional ministry. In fact, the demands upon teachers in the Evangelistic Sunday School are greater than in any other type.

And the structure of the Sunday School program must be geared to accommodate the results of the outreach. One teacher in a Primary Department related her experience. She had between 50 and 200 in her class on any given Sunday. Over 50 percent of those were new each week, because of an aggressive bus outreach program. It took more than half of the lesson time to record the names and addresses of the children. And then it was almost time to get them bundled up to leave. The leaders had planned and worked to get the children there, but they had no idea what to do with them after they arrived. And this teacher was not even aware of what was happening until after the children arrived the first week.

But the weakness that causes greatest concern is the limited depth of ministry that may characterize the Evangelistic Sunday School. If the emphasis of the church is on outreach and expansion, it is easy to neglect in-depth Bible study. Many Christians have shared with me personally that they are suffering from spiritual starvation. Dr. Gene Getz observes, "Churches that emphasize evangelism and neglect fellowship and Bible teaching are filled with people starved for the Word of God and hungry for deep relationships" *(The Sunday School Today and Tomorrow,* p. 31). Because the ministry is geared to evangelism, those already born again may be ignored. The emphasis on one part of the Great Commission (evangelism) diverts attention from the other part (teaching all of God's Word). While there may be excitement and enthusiasm, there is often little depth or maturity.

3. Educational/Fellowship Sunday Schools. The third type of

Sunday School commonly seen today is the Educational/Fellowship Sunday School. Not all Sunday Schools of this type emphasize *both* education and fellowship, but many do. We are combining these two for our consideration because both turn their focus inward, rather than reaching out and building visibility. This type of Sunday School relates to those already in the church who are following Christ.

In the Educational/Fellowship Sunday School there is a concentrated effort to minister to the members of the body of Christ, and to teach the Word of God. James Murch wrote, "The evangelical sector of the Sunday School movement has shown remarkable vitality. Great emphasis has been laid on indoctrination of the fundamentals of the Christian faith and their application to life in a changing world" *(Teach or Perish,* p. 51). There is a strong awareness of the need to help Christians mature through study of God's Word.

In order to do this, curriculum materials usually are chosen to guide students in a systematic, expository study of the Bible. Children and youth classes study appropriate passages that are applied to life. Adults may study the Bible, guided by a curriculum that leads them through the Bible in a systematic manner. Or they may meet in elective classes to study a book of the Bible in depth, or one of the excellent books available about an aspect of Christian living. The emphasis is a deeper knowledge of the Bible and its application, to help Christians live in obedience to the guidelines that have been given by God.

Frequently, these study classes also provide in-depth fellowship and sharing. A study class where a small group of Christians learn together promotes deep and meaningful fellowship. This is especially important in larger churches where it is easy to "blend in with the woodwork." Sherm Williams, pastor of Redwood Community Chapel, Castro Valley, California, described how study and fellowship are combined in his Sunday School adult classes. "One type is the 'circle class' composed of groups of eight or ten seated at a number of round tables in a large assembly room. There is a master teacher who for 30 minutes teaches the lesson or builds a foundation and framework of truth. Then the discussion leader at each table directs the interaction and discussion for 40 minutes, as application of the truth is made in a relevant manner. Each table is also a fellowship unit. The 'shepherding' process goes on through the week, with discussion leaders responsible for 'follow through'" *(The Sunday School Today and Tomorrow,* p. 18).

Ideally, fellowship should grow out of shared interests and study of the Word. In this way, the church functions as a transforming community, helping each member to come to maturity through the knowledge of the Word of God, and the support and encouragement of other believers. When the fellowship is separate from Bible study, it may or may not accomplish spiritual goals.

Another pastor related how his church meets in a non-traditional context (a restaurant) where they don't have space for Sunday School. So the Bible study/fellowship functions are provided through meeting in homes during the week. While these are not called Sunday School classes, they function in the way that effective Sunday School classes should.

And yet the Educational/Fellowship Sunday Schools are not without weaknesses. Leaders must be cautious to avoid some of the negative results that may come from this emphasis. It is easy to build a complacent ministry. Since Sunday School reflects the total church, the total ministry can become in-grown and exclusive. If the Bible is studied and applied properly, individual Christians will become aware of their responsibility to reach out to those who are unsaved. If individual Christians don't reach out, the church will lose its vitality and decline through attrition.

While the Evangelistic Sunday School may fail to emphasize in-depth Bible study, the Educational/Fellowship Sunday School may fail to emphasize evangelism, and thus become apathetic. Dr. Getz has written, "Churches that emphasize Bible teaching and fellowship but neglect evangelism often become ingrown and stagnant" *(Ibid.* p. 31).

Some members of these Sunday School classes are so taken with the warmth and satisfaction of deep and meaningful sharing that a new person finds it impossible to "break in" to the group. The classes become more like social clubs than study/sharing groups. Rather than being "salt" and "light" in the world, such groups withdraw from contact with "outsiders" and exclude all but those who are established members. Some churches even find it difficult to staff other parts of their program, because members aren't willing to give up their particular class.

No Market for Boredom

Just like people, Sunday Schools come in all shapes and sizes. And while there is great latitude in Sunday School styles, the ones that are effective are those organized to accomplish biblical goals. These goals will be considered in some depth in the next chapter.

There is no place in dynamic church ministry for the boring, uncreative program, referred to in this chapter as the Traditional Sunday School. We don't need more programs that have no goals and accomplish no purpose. We do need Sunday Schools that are planned and conducted to fulfill God's mission for the church.

We don't need Sunday Schools that bore students and cultivate negative attitudes toward the Bible. We do need Sunday Schools that teach the Word, and help students to serve God.

A Sunday School will rarely accomplish all that God intends for that church to do. Those who focus on outreach and stress evangelism will reach the unsaved and give the work of God high visibility. And yet leaders of the those Sunday Schools must be careful to provide a balanced ministry. Their new converts need to study the Bible so that they can grow and mature. Leaders must be careful to avoid a shallow ministry with superficial instruction.

Sunday Schools which emphasize instruction and/or fellowship minister to believers and help to build their biblical knowledge. Students cultivate meaningful relationships that promote unity among believers. But leaders in those Sunday Schools must avoid permitting a withdrawal attitude to be cultivated. Instead of excluding, members should seek to include others. Individual believers must be challenged to live genuine Christian lives out in the community, and to be part of the evangelistic outreach of the church. Apathy and isolation must be discouraged through Bible study and challenge to service.

When outreach and depth are rightly balanced, the Sunday School will be a vital force in producing biblical Christianity. Just as England, the United States, and other nations have been influenced and transformed through Sunday School ministry in the past, our country can again feel the effects today. When the Sunday School continues as a vital and integral part of a church ministry, people will respond as those in the first century who ". . . turned to God from idols to serve a living and true God" (1 Thes. 1:9).

9
The Mission
of the Church

God has divinely established the Church universal. Christ promised that He would build His Church, and that it would be more powerful than its opposition. Even the gates of hell, or the very power of Satan himself, would not be able to overcome it. Those who support the Church identify with the purposes of Christ. Those who oppose the Church identify with the purposes of Satan. (See Matt. 16:18-19.)

In this discussion of the mission of the Church, when *Church* is capitalized, it means the universal body of Christ. A lowercase *church* refers to a local fellowship of believers.

Sunday School as Part of the Church

The Sunday School is of human origin and not a program specifically mandated by God. Because it is only one of several instructional agencies, a program such as Sunday School cannot be evaluated by itself. Like all other ministries of the church, it must be appraised in the context of the Church's mission. In order to do this, we must make a two-step assessment. The first step is to consider what the Church is, and what God intends for it to accomplish. This means examining the biblical guidelines.

The second step is to determine whether or not the Sunday School is a program that strengthens the Church to accomplish those purposes that God has for it. If Sunday School strengthens and promotes the Church, it is valid. If it does not, then there is no need to continue on to administration of the Sunday School program.

Only after these two steps have been taken can leaders concentrate on planning and running a Sunday School program. Unfortunately, many leaders in local churches skip these two steps. They never consider the overall emphasis and purpose of the Church, and fail to determine whether Sunday School is an asset or a liability. They concentrate on the functional details of administrating a program.

When church leaders concentrate on administration, without considering the two prior steps, various problems and distortions occur. Some leaders may develop a blind loyalty to a program, although that program has little to do with accomplishing the biblical mission of the Church. Others may oppose the same program if they think it is extraneous to the work of that church. When the basic purpose of the Church is ignored, leaders may organize and plan activities that compete with other ministries of the church.

When the two evaluative steps have been carefully considered, effective administration follows naturally. If Christians know why the Church exists (step one), and they understand how the Sunday School is an integral part of the Church's mission (step two), then the Sunday School program has all the potential of being a powerful force in the life and ministry of a local church. When the evaluative steps have been taken, teachers will come prepared. They will know what is expected of them, and what they should expect of themselves. They will feel an excitement and enthusiasm that a purposeless program, conducted because of tradition, can never generate. And this enthusiasm will be excitement about participating in the work of God in the world and in the church.

Teachers are crying for this vision. In many churches teachers are so committed to God that they have been serving for years without really knowing why they are working in the Sunday School, or if they are doing a good job. This smoldering flame of commitment needs only to be encouraged to burst into a fire for God. But we must lead ourselves and those working in our churches through steps one and two. Then we can conduct Sunday Schools that are a vital part of the ministry of the church. Let's consider the elements included in step one.

Step One—Biblical Guidelines

The only way that we possibly can understand what the Church ought to be is by consulting the biblical guidelines. Many churches are structured, and their programs conducted, with no consideration given to what Christ intended His Church to be. A local church may have many people in attendance or it may have few. It may have Sunday School or it may not. It may be traditional or innovative. And yet, these factors do not determine whether or not a church is biblical.

Some people have the idea that church growth proves God's blessing. But Sunday activities other than church can draw vast crowds. Drive past a football stadium for an obvious example. Other people have the idea that small churches are pure. But some of the least biblical churches around are small, weak, and ineffective. Neither *large* nor *small* has anything necessarily in common with *biblical.*

Some people may have the idea that a particular style of worship service is what counts. Some prefer a formal liturgy; others, an informal. Preferring the formal liturgy is neither more nor less biblical than preferring the informal. Some feel that the more services held each week, the better, while others maintain that all services and activities should be planned for one, or at the most, two days each week

A problem with all of these measurements of a church's effectiveness is the focus on superficial issues. Members major in peripheral issues, and fail to consider the significant biblical guidelines. While it is true that all of the matters mentioned here bear some relationship to being biblical, these measurements are really the effect and not the cause.

The principles that really are significant influence and permeate all programming and activities. These are the guidelines for the mission of the Church which determine how a local church can fulfill that mission. Leaders must understand the basic principles, so that they can make programming and administrative decisions based on these principles. These principles are relevant to all cultures, in all periods of time.

1. The biblical concept of the Church. The most literal rendering of the Greek word for *Church* is a "called-out group." This describes all of those who have accepted Jesus Christ as Saviour. They have been called out of the world, and are now members of a single group, the Church. This group is described as a *body,* with Christ as the head (Eph. 4:14-16; 1 Cor. 12:12-27). The Church also is described as a *bride* (Rev. 21:2, 9), a *building* in which the individual parts are believers (Eph. 2:19-21), a *holy nation* (1 Peter 2:9), a *chosen race* (1 Peter 2:9), a *royal priesthood* (1 Peter 2:9).

Many of the descriptions of the Church are plural. This is because the Church, the body of Christ, is made up of many different parts. All of these parts ought to be working together to bring the group and all members in it to full maturity. It is unfortunate that some Christians develop a "Lone Ranger complex," feeling that they are fighting against the world all by themselves. God has brought us together into a group, a called-out group, so that we may work together to accomplish His work in the world.

The basic concept of the Church is that it is a single group, or body, made up of many different parts. This body must work together cooperatively, under the direction of the Head, Jesus Christ, in order to fulfill His purposes.

A local church is a group of believers who live in general proximity to each other, and who have committed themselves to work together. This is a visible expression of the relationship that all believers have to each other. The word *fellowship* has often been used to describe a local group of believers functioning this way. Fellowship implies different individuals all working together or relating to each other. The local church is a fellowship of believers functioning under the direction of Jesus Christ.

2. The biblical qualities of the Church. We must go beyond the basic concept and consider some of the distinguishing qualities of this fellowship. In *The Church at the End of the 20th Century,* Francis Schaeffer has written that the distinguishing mark of the Christian must be love. Christ has commanded it, and the Church is to demonstrate it (InterVarsity Press, 1970, Appendix II, pp. 133-153).

But what about characteristics of Christians interacting within a local church? There must be certain qualities that characterize believers in fellowship together.

Gene Getz, in *Sharpening the Focus of the Church,* suggested that the three qualities of a mature church are faith, hope, and love. "This is quite clear from Paul's writings, since he frequently used these three virtues to measure the maturity level of the New Testament churches" (Moody Press, 1974, p. 53). If indeed these are distinguishing qualities of the Church, then each local church should plan its program and activities to promote the development of these traits and qualities. Dr. Getz summarized the mature and immature qualities of a fellowship of believers. An immature church "reflects impatience, jealousy, strife, divisions, pride, arrogance, and unbecoming behavior. If it is mature, it reflects a growing love, a unity of faith, and a steadfast hope" *(Ibid.,* p. 61).

But what is it that produces these marks of maturity in a group of believers? The Apostle Paul gave the answer to that question. In his concern about the maturity of the Thessalonian Church, he emphasized two specific ways that he worked to build that maturity. The first of these was to communicate the truth to them. He wrote and spoke what God had said. Paul wrote, "But just as we have been approved by God to be entrusted with the Gospel, so we speak, not as pleasing men but God, who examines our hearts" (1 Thes. 2:4).

There is no way that believers can mature unless they know the Word of God. God has communicated to us, and our spiritual maturity—the demonstration of faith, hope, and love—can only come as a result of receiving and understanding that truth from God.

Christians who are ignorant of the Bible are immature Christians. Spiritual growth cannot thrive in an atmosphere of biblical ignorance. The first way to build spiritual maturity among Christians is to teach them the Word of God.

But there is also a second way in which Paul worked to build maturity in the Thessalonian Church. Not only did he speak and write the truth to them, but he also established meaningful relationships. Paul wrote, "But we proved to be gentle among you, as a nursing mother tenderly cares for her own children. Having thus a fond affection for you, we were well-pleased to impart to you not only the Gospel of God but also our own lives, because you had become very dear to us" (1 Thes. 2:7-8).

Paul knew that a relationship had to be established between himself and those to whom he was ministering. This had to be a relationship of love, and trust, and total commitment. So he shared himself with the Thessalonians. He acted first as a mother.

He then compared this relationship to the way a father relates to his children. "You are witnesses, and so is God, how devoutly and uprightly and blamelessly we behaved toward you believers; just as you know how we were exhorting and encouraging and imploring each one of you as a father would his own children, so that you may walk in a manner worthy of the God who calls you into His own kingdom and glory" (1 Thes. 2:10-12).

Paul also knew that it was not enough to share the truth in some cold, abstract, logical sort of manner. He realized that a relationship of trust and concern had to be established. And so he worked very hard to share more than his knowledge. He shared himself, his love, his feeling, and his affections, as a parent does. As he helped the believers grow and mature, they increasingly became a fellowship of Christians who demonstrated faith, hope, and love.

Faith, hope, and love are not qualities that appear simply because a group of people meet together and choose to incorporate themselves as a local church. These qualities only come about as the activities of that group promote such qualities. The activities or program must provide for instruction in the Word of God. And the program must also provide opportunities for mature Christian teachers to share themselves with their students.

• *Faith* cannot be built on ignorance, because faith must have an *object*. When a person believes, he has to believe in something. There must be a content to faith. When a person has faith in Jesus Christ, it ought to mean that he believes the facts about Christ as taught in the Bible. But that concept is meaningless if he does not know the content of the Bible.

Faith is also encouraged and promoted by meaningful *contact* with Christians who are practicing faith. Ideally, the person who teaches the content of faith also demonstrates the practice of faith. When a person teaches the facts of biblical faith to another, he also needs the opportunity to demonstrate that faith by his own life. Good church programming includes both elements.

• *Hope* is based on the revealed Word of God. No matter how

Col 224

bleak the future seems and how bad the present situation is, the Christian has a reason to hope. The return of Jesus Christ and the promise of God's strength have generated hope in Christians for centuries. For hope exists when Christians know what God has said to give them reason for their hope.

But hope is more than a theological certainty. Hope ought to be a practical dimension in our lives. When circumstances look bad and the future seems worse, the Christian with God's perspective can demonstrate the practical outworking of hope by how he lives. This is not a blind optimism, but rather a realistic anticipation of God actively working in the world. Hope needs a factual basis, but it also must be demonstrated in concrete ways.

• *Love* is usually misinterpreted in our culture. When most people use the word *love,* they mean some sort of physical or emotional feeling. But that is not the biblical definition of the quality of love in the Church. Biblical love is an act of the will. It is choosing to do something for another person because it is good for him. It means seeking the best for another. Jesus Christ did not die for us because He *felt* like doing it, but because He chose to sacrifice Himself for us. A teacher ought to prepare to teach a Sunday School class, not because it makes him happy, but because he has chosen to act on the basis of the welfare of that class. The highest application of love in a local church can only be understood as we know what God has said about love.

And yet, as much as faith and hope, love has to be visible in everyday life. Children don't learn that their parents love them because the parents tell them so. Children know that they are loved by how the parents act toward them. Immature Christians don't learn how to relate to other members of the body of Christ by studying the Word of God in a vacuum. They need to see Christian love put into practice by those more mature Christians in the fellowship of their church.

So what are the implications for churches today? We know that it is important to cultivate the qualities of faith, hope, and love. But this has to be a two-part process. The Bible needs to be taught; for only as the truth of the Bible is taught, will faith, hope, and love be understood in their true biblical meanings. These meanings cannot be learned from secular sources.

But even more than the facts, the demonstration of faith, hope, and love has to be learned, and it can only be learned through relationships. Effective church programming must include instruction in the Word and in the demonstration of faith, hope, and love.

3. The biblical tasks of the Church. We have to think beyond the qualities that should be evident in the life of the Church to the tasks that God has assigned to the Church. Rather than looking at many passages, we will consider only one, since it represents both the mission of the Church and the method of accomplishing that mission.

After His resurrection, Jesus Christ commissioned His followers to continue the ministry that He had begun: "Go therefore and make disciples of all the nations, baptizing them in the name of the Father and the Son and the Holy Spirit, teaching them to observe all that I command you; and lo, I am with you always, even to the end of the age" (Matt. 28:19-20).

While this is generally a good translation, it could be improved slightly. The first part of verse 19 could be more accurately translated, "Therefore, going, make disciples of all the nations. . . ." The advantage of this translation is that it relates precisely what Christ said. Christ gave one command to His followers: "Make disciples." And there are three words describing how to do it. The process of making disciples is described by the "ing" words (Greek participles) "going," "baptizing," and "teaching."

• Fulfilling the command to make disciples involves three things. The first of these is *going*. This implies availability. Christ did not specify where His followers were to go. The conclusion is that they ought to make disciples wherever they were led by God. It was to be a habit. This was to be a general lifestyle.

• The second element in making disciples is *baptizing*. When a person was baptized in the New Testament Church, he publicly stated that he had accepted Christ. In many churches today a person is asked to come forward to demonstrate that he accepts Christ. In the New Testament period, baptism included the concept that we call evangelizing.

• The third element in making disciples is *teaching* all that God has communicated. Jesus Christ instructed His followers to teach the new converts not just to know, but to observe (practice) all that He had taught. It is not enough to lead a person to Christ and forget him.

That person must then be taught the Word of God. And he must be taught in such a way that he will not merely add theoretical knowledge, but will experience a change in his daily behavior.

It should be a great encouragement for us to realize that Christ concluded His command with a promise. He promised that His followers would not have to do all of this alone. As they were going, evangelizing, and teaching, He would be with them, even to the end of the age.

This is the mission assigned to the Church today. We are to make disciples. This means to help persons accept Christ and then mature in their spiritual walk. Wherever we happen to be, we must evangelize and teach. The effective church stresses the responsibility of each believer to be involved in the work of evangelizing and/or teaching. This involvement is for all Christians. The distinction between lay persons and clergy did not exist in the New Testament. Certain members of the body have been given leadership gifts. But these leaders can never take the place of total lay involvement.

Having a paid pastor or other staff member is neither commanded nor forbidden. However, the involvement of all Christians in ministry activity is commanded. Lay ministry is the heart and life of the church. And it is only as individual lay persons are mobilized that the effective work of making disciples will be accomplished.

Applying the principles that we have considered in this chapter will assist a local fellowship of believers to determine whether their church is functioning in accordance with the Word of God. The principles must be applied if we hope to cultivate the life qualities that should be present in the church. A church is to be characterized by faith, hope, and love. But these traits can only be cultivated by teaching the Word of God and by building relationships through programs like Sunday School. These tasks have to be done by lay persons, on a churchwide scale.

The principles in this chapter also apply to accomplishing the tasks of the Church. We can do this through programming that is designed to make disciples by evangelizing and teaching. And the way to accomplish the Church's tasks is the same way we cultivate biblical qualities. We must teach the content of the Bible, and build biblical relationships. Making disciples must involve all Christians, for this is the task of the Church.

Step Two

The last three chapters of this book deal with the second step in designing Sunday School ministries that will both build biblical qualities and accomplish the biblical tasks for the Church. These chapters will focus on the place of Sunday School in building a church program. We will look at the unique characteristics of a Sunday School program and determine how they contribute to building a strong church. We will consider the importance of teaching the Bible, the importance of building meaningful relationships through groups, and the importance of mobilizing a vast force of lay persons.

10
Sunday School
and the Bible

Sunday School ought to be one of a church's strongest programs. It can contribute to the ministry of the church only as it is seen in the context of the mission of the church, and as the leaders help all church members understand the role Sunday School plays.

But the actual process of building a strong Sunday School takes dedication and work. There are three lessons that we can learn from our brief review of the progress of the Sunday School movement. Each of these last three chapters focuses on one of these three lessons.

Emphasize the Bible

The first lesson that we need to learn is that Sunday School can be successful only when it is characterized by effective teaching that emphasizes the Bible. The content of the Sunday School curriculum has to be the absolute truth of God's Word. The beginning of the recorded decline in Sunday School attendance corresponded with the liberal emphasis in curriculum materials. During this period the Bible content in the materials was replaced with other emphases.

James D. Murch wrote, "Pure Christianity has always insisted on an educated constituency—one that knows basic doctrine, why Christian beliefs are superior to other beliefs, that knows its basic ethical code and is intent on winning others to Christ" *(Teach or Perish,* p. 64). When this knowledge of biblical content is weak,

Christianity is weak. When Christians are illiterate, they are immature, and the church will be fragmented and ineffective.

The Apostle Paul stressed the need for Bible knowledge in 2 Timothy 3:16-17: "All Scripture is inspired by God and profitable for teaching, for reproof, for correction, for training in righteousness; that the man of God may be adequate, equipped for every good work." Notice that Paul identified four specific contributions of the Bible. It is profitable for teaching, for reproof, for correction, for training in righteousness.

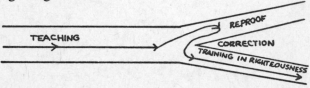

If we were to picture the Christian life as a journey along a road with a fork in it, we could plot these four categories of profitability on that road. The first function, *teaching,* is to help us know what direction we should take. It is the basic guidance in living the Christian life.

But we must make a decision when confronted with a fork in the road. Suppose God wants us to take the right-hand road when we come to the fork, but instead we take the left-hand road. This is where the second function comes into play. The Word is profitable for *reproof,* that is, telling us when we have made a wrong decision, and when we have gotten sidetracked.

However, once we know that we have made a mistake, we have to get back on the right road. This is where the third function of the Bible can be experienced. Scripture is profitable for *correction.* Correction is helping us get back on the right road once we have recognized our error.

Finally, after getting back on the right road, we need to continue making progress along the way. The fourth function of the Bible relates to that continued progress. After heading in the right direction, finding out that we made a wrong turn, and then getting back on the right road, Scripture is profitable for *training in righteousness.* The Bible helps us continue to make progress in righteous living.

The end result of this application of Scripture is that the Christian will be adequate to do what God desires. He will be equipped to do the good works that God expects. But these experiences will be impossible without a knowledge of the content of the Bible.

Sunday School must stress teaching the entire Bible. It is only as Christians teach the Word that they fulfill the commands of God. Paul emphasized in the previous chapter (2 Tim. 2:2) that it is the responsibility of a Christian to pass along to others the things that he has learned from the Word of God. As the church instructs its members, it becomes a vital growing church.

Two Answers to Criticism

One of the accusations sometimes directed against Christian educators is that we instruct persons, especially children, in truths that they are not ready to apply to life. Some claim that by stressing the importance of biblical facts, we teach concepts that will not be applied directly until the students grow older.

Such criticism may grow out of a philosophy of experience-based education. This is a philosophy that maintains that education ought not to be preparation for life, as much as it ought to be life itself. Such a philosophy is based on a naturalistic approach to education and may deny the existence of moral and other absolutes.

Commitment to the inspired Word of God provides us with two responses to the accusation that we teach students before they are ready to apply the principles to their lives. The first of these responses is theological, the second, philosophical.

1. Theological. Jesus Christ, the Master Teacher, instructed His disciples in preparation for what He knew they would experience in the future. As Jesus was preparing His disciples for His crucifixion, He shared the teachings of the prophets about the Crucifixion, and how those things were going to be accomplished. But in Luke 18:34 we read, "And they understood none of these things, and this saying was hidden from them, and they did not comprehend the things that were said."

Unquestionably, Christ knew what their response was going to be. He knew that they would be confused after the class session, and He still chose to share the truth with them. Stranger yet, He didn't pause and go over the lesson again until they understood. He chose to tell them and leave them in confusion, wondering what it all meant.

Now this is not to encourage Sunday School teachers to confuse students or leave them bewildered after class. It is to emphasize that under certain circumstances, students need to know something even though the full implications will not be perceived until a later time.

Christ taught His disciples, knowing that the Holy Spirit would later take the truths that had been shared and remind the disciples of them. Then they would be able to handle themselves in the midst of difficulty. This reliance upon the teaching ministry of the Holy Spirit is explained in John 14:26: "But the Helper, the Holy Spirit, whom the Father will send in My name, He will teach you all things, and bring to your remembrance all that I said to you."

There is value in teaching children the Bible. There is inestimable value in Bible memorization. It is only as children and adults know Bible truths that the Holy Spirit can use these truths to guide and direct them at some later date. This is not to say we should make our teaching irrelevant. We must do everything possible to apply the Word, to help our students see how it relates to their lives. But in the final analysis, we must prepare students for the future.

The balance between immediate and long-range application is demonstrated in Titus 2:11-13. Paul told Titus that instruction would help believers live sensibly, righteously, and godly in the present age. That is the immediate application. But he also taught that instruction would help them look toward the blessed hope of the future return of the Lord Jesus. In verse 15 Paul wrote, "These things speak and exhort and reprove with all authority. Let no one disregard you." We teach the Bible, and we teach it with authority. We teach the Bible both for immediate application, and for the Holy Spirit to apply at an appropriate later date.

2. Philosophical. The second response to the accusation that we teach students before they are ready to apply the truth is, "That's right, we do!" But that's the way it ought to be. For if we believe in absolutes, then we must also believe that there are right and wrong ways to act in certain situations. And students have to know what God has said, so that they can choose the right and avoid the wrong. We can further assert that most of the really important decisions in life will be made on the basis of earlier knowledge, or prior decisions.

If I plan to attend a seminar on death and dying and other crises in life, I am not going because I expect to die there. I don't expect the person next to me to die either. But I expect that I and others close to me will face these situations sometime in the future. It is too late to prepare to counsel another when that person is on the verge of death. And so I must prepare ahead of time.

It would be great if, when a young couple were seated in the back of a car parked on a deserted road, their Sunday School teacher could be in the front seat to guide them in making decisions. But that's not the way it happens. Moral choices almost always are made on the basis of decisions made earlier in a neutral context. It is the ministry of the Holy Spirit to remind a young man or woman, tempted to sin, of the biblical experience of Joseph (Gen. 39). The Holy Spirit will bring back the Word of God if it has been learned previously. But the Christian who doesn't know the Bible has frustrated the aim of the Holy Spirit, because he has not given God's Spirit any ammunition with which to work.

The employee tempted to steal from his employer will be ministered to by the Holy Spirit if he has learned the teaching of God's Word. (See Ephesians 4:28; Proverbs 11:1; Exodus 20:15.) The pastor or Sunday School teacher will not be there to help resist temptation. But the Holy Spirit will remind that employee of what he has learned. Sadly, many Christians don't have this advantage because they have failed to study the Bible. They don't know what God has said.

Study Biblical Doctrine

In order to gain maximum value from our knowledge of the Bible, we must know more than isolated facts. This is where the importance of high quality, biblical curriculum materials becomes evident. In 1 Peter 3:15-16, Christians are admonished always to be prepared to answer their accusers. When someone wants to know what makes a Christian tick, why he lives the way he does, that Christian needs to have an answer. And the answer is an articulation of a Christian philosophy of life, of a lifestyle based on God's Word. But in order to do this, the Christian must understand how various parts of Scripture are related. This is doctrine.

I grow exasperated with those who maintain that we don't need to know doctrine, but only need to know Jesus. Some claim we need to know the Bible, but not doctrine. Ridiculous! We cannot know Jesus without knowing doctrine.

Anytime two Bible truths are related, we immediately have doctrine. To know that "all have sinned," is to know a Bible fact. To know that "all have sinned" and also that "the wages of sin is death," is to know doctrine. When two Bible truths are connected, we have an elementary doctrinal statement.

Systematic teaching is doctrinal teaching. Now this doesn't mean that a Sunday School class should sound like a public reading of a volume of systematic theology. But it does mean that we must teach more than isolated Bible facts. When we teach that Jesus Christ is God's Son, we are teaching a Bible fact. When we teach that Jesus Christ died, we are teaching a Bible fact. When we teach that Jesus Christ the Son of God died, we are teaching an elementary doctrine of Christ, Christology.

After the Resurrection, Jesus met two disciples on the road to Emmaus. They were totally disillusioned and defeated by the recent events of the Crucifixion. In Luke 24:27 we read, "And beginning with Moses and with all the prophets, He explained to them the things concerning Himself in all the Scriptures." That was doctrine. And doctrine such as mortal man has never heard, before or since. A doctrinal exposition about Christ, and by Christ.

The commentary found a few verses later in Luke 24:32 gives us insight into their response. "And they said to one another, 'Were not our hearts burning within us while He was speaking to us on the road, while He was explaining the Scriptures to us?'" Of course their hearts were warmed to the boiling point. They were comprehending part of the system of Scripture, the perfect system communicated by the Perfect Communicator. While we are incomplete in our doctrinal comprehension, doctrine taught and applied will warm the hearts of the hearers. We don't need less doctrine. We need more! And it must be biblical!

When the church fails to encourage effective doctrinal study and teaching, it is easy for error to creep in. If Christians don't have a systematic grasp of biblical truths they will be slow to detect heresy. A phenomenon which is enjoying current popularity is caring/sharing groups. But when these groups ignore basic doctrinal truths, they can become the seedbeds of divisiveness and potential heresy. When a church provides small-group Bible study (through Sunday School or other study groups), that church can provide these caring/sharing experiences, and will be functioning as a church ought to. Pastor Sherman Williams has stated, "The small group formula can only know lasting value if these groups are anchored to absolute truth and to the Church, the body of Christ" *(The Sunday School Today and Tomorrow,* p. 17).

Communicate Effectively

So if we really want our Sunday Schools to make a significant contribution to the life of the church, we must begin by teaching the Bible. And we must teach it systematically, utilizing comprehensive biblical curriculum materials. But there is a corollary to this concept. We must also employ effective techniques of communication. For teaching that obscures truth is worse than no teaching at all.

Teachers need resources to enable them to teach effectively and communicate clearly. A teacher who is committed to doing an excellent job will be delighted when high quality resources are provided by the church. But unfortunately, good resources will not compensate for a lazy teacher. And many times students are bored or confused by poorly prepared teachers.

1. Preparation. One curriculum publisher conducted a study to determine the average length of time spent in preparation by teachers using their materials. The report was that the average teacher spent just 15 minutes in preparation. This means that if the class were 45 minutes long, the teacher prepared 3 times faster than he taught! This is hardly the attitude of the apostles recorded in Acts 6:2: "It is not desirable for us to neglect the Word of God in order to serve tables." So they appointed men to care for those other functions and concluded in Acts 6:4: "But we will devote ourselves to prayer, and to the ministry of the Word." The teacher spending 15 minutes a week in preparation does not expect to see the results that the apostles experienced.

Frank E. Gaebelein concluded, "Christians today are notoriously lazy-minded. Too often the Protestant layman relies solely upon his minister for the understanding and, if the truth be told, even for the reading of his Bible" *(The Pattern of God's Truth,* Moody Press, 1960, p. 45).

This laziness is nowhere more evident than in the Sunday School classroom. Curriculum publishers are finding it necessary to simplify lesson materials because teachers are not willing to take the time to prepare deeply.

2. Methodology. One outcome of adequate preparation is effective teaching methodology. To be truly effective in Sunday School teaching, a teacher must take advantage of the opportunities that are available for group interaction. There are many methods that can be used to secure active involvement. Discussion, question/answer, and other methods that draw out student response are ideally suited to Sunday School instruction. George Herbert wrote many years ago in the *Country Parson,* "At sermons and at prayers men may sleep or wander, but when one is asked a question, he must disclose what he is" (Trumbull, *Yale Lectures,* p. 91).

Imagine being invited to dinner by a friend. As you enter the dining room, the table is graciously set with china and silver. On the table are lighted candles. Following the appetizer of tomato juice and crackers, is the main course of juicy broiled sirloin steak. Baked potatoes with sour cream and chives, and a crisp salad with bleu cheese dressing are served. There are fresh rolls with butter and an assortment of tasty relishes. All of these are served with the greatest care. Following the meal is homemade apple pie with ice cream, and freshly brewed coffee. What a delightful experience!

Consider the same meal handed to you in a pail. In that pail are the sirloin steak and the candles, the tomato juice and crackers. The salad with dressing, the potatoes with sour cream, and the rolls, butter, and relishes have been dumped in. Finally, your friend has added the homemade apple pie, ice cream, and coffee. All of the nourishment is there. The excellent ingredients with all of their unique tastes, and even the candles, are included. And yet the manner of presentation totally destroys the effect, and probably your appetite too.

Good methodology employed in teaching can never compensate for lack of content. Unless the content of the Bible is taught, the class will have limited value. And yet, even when the content of the Bible is included, poor preparation and methodology can limit the effectiveness of teaching the Word of God.

Unfortunately, a note found in the wastebasket of an eighth grade classroom in Philadelphia characterizes some Christian education classes. The note read, "How can you stay awake, I'm so bored I could lie down on the floor and go to sleep. I don't see how she can talk so much. I wish she would let us talk sometimes." Some have suggested that some teachers may be guilty of intellectual homicide because many of them talk their students to death.

Christians, more than anyone else, should be committed to the value of effective teaching. Since we have the most important message in the world, our methodology should be regarded as important too. We dare not be lazy in our preparation or our teaching. While we have every right to expect God to bless the results of our teaching, we also ought to follow the laws of communication that He has created.

Just because I am a Christian doesn't mean that I have the right to plant a crop of corn in Illinois in late December and blame God for no harvest. If I want to harvest corn, I must follow God's laws of agriculture. The same is true with teaching. A Christian teacher who knows and follows the laws of communication can expect God's blessing.

The Bible is the most important content in the world, and it has to be the basis of all Sunday School instruction. With a message so important, it is imperative that we devote adequate time and planning to our teaching so that the message of the Bible can be communicated as effectively as possible.

11
Sunday School and
the Personal Touch

Sunday School is not dead! It has played a vital role in the growth and development of the Church for 200 years. But while it is alive, its health leaves something to be desired. Unfortunately, for some people Sunday School has become a routine exercise, lacking in purpose and vitality.

In order to avoid this, we must look carefully at the purpose of Sunday School to see how it fits into the total church program. Only as Sunday School contributes to accomplishing the mandate that Christ gave His church, can it be promoted as a valid program. Christ commanded the church to make followers of Him, by leading people to a saving faith in Him, and then teaching them Bible truths (doctrine).

However, even if we know the purpose of the Sunday School, and how it functions as a vital element in discipling persons, we still may conduct ineffective Sunday Schools. In the last chapter we considered the first lesson that grows out of the history of the Sunday School movement. Teachers who do not know the Word of God, or who are inadequately trained, will frustrate the ministry.

However, it is possible to have a properly conceived Sunday School, staffed with teachers who are prepared to communicate effectively, and still conduct an ineffective Sunday School. Effective Sunday School teaching demands far more than prepared Christian teaching and Bible-based curriculum.

Commitment to Self-Giving

The second lesson that history should teach us is that effective Sunday Schools demand teachers who are committed to sharing themselves personally with their students in the context of the life of the church. This means building a quality of relationship that extends far beyond the allotted lesson time on Sunday morning. Actually, the *attitude* of wanting to build relationships with students may be even more important than how well a teacher is able to instruct his students in class.

Consider a teacher who is spiritually mature, who loves the students in his class, and deeply desires to relate to them personally. He is concerned about them and is willing to spend time with them to help them become mature Christians. But he is not a very good teacher. He is poorly organized and doesn't use very good methodology. In fact he is a boring lecturer.

On the other hand consider a teacher who is technically competent in the classroom. He knows effective teaching techniques. His sessions sparkle with creativity. He teaches from a well-designed lesson plan and is logical and concise in his instruction. But he sees teaching as doing something *for* the class. He comes to class to "teach the lesson," and leaves class feeling he has done his job. He is more concerned about the lesson than he is about the students.

It is obvious which of these teachers will have the long-term impact on his class. Teaching is far more than sharing facts—it is sharing of oneself. While this point may seem obvious, many people fail to recognize it as obvious in the Sunday School classroom. Recently, I read a statement to the effect that not being taken to Sunday School was probably a blessing, because later in life, there were no false ideas about the Bible to unlearn. Granted, this may be true in some Sunday Schools. However, it certainly should not be stated as a generalized principle. Even when the Bible is taught accurately, the knowledge gained is only part of the benefit for the child. Significant relationships can be built at an early age with concerned adults outside of a child's immediate family, and the child can sense the caring that ought to be a primary quality of the church.

When my family and I would drive past our church, whether it was Sunday or not, our preschool children would become excited. Even before they could talk, they were delighted when they saw our church.

This was not due to all the profound things they were learning there, but because there was a group of teachers who cared for them. They knew they were loved. They were loved by other members of the body of Christ, and I don't want them ever to forget that lesson. The church and meaningful relationships with concerned Christians ought to be a normal part of life for every Christian, at as early an age as possible.

Relationship-Building

Many churches find it difficult to staff the preschool departments. After all, who wants to come to the church and "baby-sit"? If we have problems in staffing the Nursery and Toddler Departments, it may be because we have failed to expand the vision of our workers to see the value of relationship-building. These relationships often will be far more meaningful in later life than the facts that were learned in class.

Larry Richards has suggested that one of the weaknesses in many Sunday Schools is an excessive reliance on the school model of education. We have tried to pattern Sunday Schools after other educational institutions. He has observed that the relationship with the community is the real educator, and that building a "transforming community" should be more important than the "administration of a schooling institution" *(Religious Education* 74, no. 1, January-February, 1979).

It's terribly important that we not forget the emphasis of the previous chapter as we consider this dimension of Sunday School. The facts of the Word of God remain a top priority. We must teach students so that they learn what God has communicated. And yet we dare not stop with the transmission of facts. We must continue to help students become what God wants them to become. But this aspect of learning demands meaningful relationships between teacher and student.

Jesus Christ's ministry upon the earth lasted for only three years. And yet in those three years, He laid the groundwork for a movement that would sweep around the world and revolutionize earthly institutions. Christ's strategy was to choose a few select men and equip them to carry out His mission in the world. In spite of facing incalculable odds and having limited time, Christ accomplished His mission.

The key element in Christ's strategy was to build relationships. Mark recorded Christ's approach in his Gospel, Mark 3:13-15. Verse 13 is a summary statement of the fact that Christ called the disciples and they followed Him. The next two verses describe the three things the disciples were called to do.

The disciples were called to be with Christ; they were called to preach; and they were given authority to cast out demons. Notice that the first thing Christ wanted to do with His disciples was to build a relationship. They were to be with Him. This meant getting to know each other personally. It could not be a superficial, spend-an-hour-together-each-week kind of relationship. But the relationship included a sharing of ideas, values, goals, and failures. It was a relationship based on love and acceptance where each learned how to communicate freely, honestly, and openly with the others, sharing who he really was.

And the result was that the disciples increasingly became like Christ. This is the genius of discipleship. Luke 6:40 relates Christ's instruction on the subject of teaching through a parable. In this lesson Christ shared that, ". . . everyone, after he has been fully trained, will be like his teacher." Jesus Christ spent time with His disciples so that they could get to know Him well enough to build a deep and meaningful relationship.

Dr. Richard Halverson, internationally known Christian leader, was quoted in *Christianity Today,* August 18, 1967. He said, "I think this is fundamental to an effective Sunday School, that the teacher relate to persons, and I consider this relationship with persons fundamental to effectiveness as a teacher." He further explained, "Relating means involving oneself with those children in the totality of their lives all through the week instead of just unloading a lesson on them in the Sunday School classroom and then letting them go" (p. 10).

The quality of relationships that are built between teacher and student largely determines the effectiveness of instruction. While the content of the Bible is of critical importance in Sunday School teaching, the relationships that are developed often determine the long-term effectiveness of the lessons. In fact many people remember the relationships far more explicitly than the lesson content. Such is true in my experience.

A Personal Memory

My parents saw to it that I attended Sunday School regularly, and they attended with me. But as I look back upon those early Sunday School experiences, I remember persons more than facts.

• I remember attending Sunday School when I was in the Primary Department. We probably participated in interesting learning activities. There must have been visual aids, and interesting stories, interest centers, and visualized songs. Bible facts were taught and application was made. And yet, I've forgotten those things.

But I do remember a teacher who loved me. She was interested in me and concerned about me. She communicated that love in such a way that almost 30 years later I still remember that she loved me. I don't remember what she taught, but I remember the relationship. I remember Mrs. Harvey Hiles.

• I remember attending Sunday School when I was in the Junior Department. Actually, I remember more about my experiences in the Junior Department than in the Primary Department, partly because I was older, and partly because of how I was involved. I remember a teacher with incredible patience, when we acted like grade-school boys, or worse.

The class arrangement was not conducive to effective education to begin with. We all sat around a long table made of three wide boards with open cracks between them. And our teacher sat at the end. When we all leaned forward, with our shoulders against the table, no arm motion was visible. And all six boys would gaze with innocent expressions of wonder as pieces of paper would mysteriously emerge through the cracks in the table, only to disappear as the teacher grabbed for them and then reappear at another place on the table.

I remember what was underneath that table. The bottom was covered with so many wads of gum that it felt more like a gravel driveway than a table bottom. After all, we wouldn't think of chewing gum in Sunday School! And I remember the active trading that went on under the table. Trading of the wonderful and strange things that can be found in the pockets of sixth-grade boys.

But more than these things, I remember a man—a quiet gentle man who would get frustrated at the antics of the boys he loved. It probably was not very evident that we were learning. But we were. The dedication and commitment of that teacher was apparent to us.

And we learned, not so much from what he said, but from what he was. I remember a teacher who loved me. I remember J. Rollin Ewen.

• I remember attending Sunday School when I was in the Junior High Department. That's when the statistics indicate we were supposed to drop out of Sunday School. And some of us may have considered doing just that. But our parents decided otherwise. I only remember one specific thing that was said in that class. And I remember that because I argued with it. But I learned as a junior high student. I learned that we had a pastor who, in spite of being busy, was concerned about us.

In addition to his preaching and pastoral duties, he accepted a teaching assignment. He accepted the class because he was concerned. And he communicated this concern. We knew he loved us. And because of that we loved him too. And so we respected him for what he was. We learned from him—from his Sunday School lessons and from his sermons, but mainly from his life. I don't specifically remember the content of those lessons or sermons. But I do remember a relationship that was built. I remember Rev. James N. McCoy.

Provision for a Personal Touch

You see, Sunday School's value extends beyond the facts that are communicated. You cannot have an effective Bible teaching ministry without teaching those facts. But in order to gain maximum benefit, meaningful relationships must be cultivated in the process. The Rev. Sherm Williams affirmed this concept. "The genius of the Sunday School is the provision for the personal touch. There must be a 'rub-off' from teacher to pupil. His life must incarnate the truth he teaches. The 'shepherding' concept is basic to the success of the Sunday School" *(The Sunday School Today and Tomorrow, p. 18).*

In *The Pattern of God's Truth,* a book that has profound insights for Christian educators, Frank E. Gaebelein stressed the importance of the teacher. "In one way or another, every teacher expresses the convictions he lives by, whether they be spiritually positive or negative" (p. 37). He was applying this concept to formal education institutions, but it applies to all Christian education. The quality of the spiritual commitment of the teacher determines the quality of

Christian education. For the teacher communicates by what he *is* far more than by what he *says*. He communicates by relationships.

Dr. Howard Hendricks, dean of Christian educators, frequently relates the impact that a Sunday School teacher had upon his life. He describes how a man with little formal education took a personal interest in each of the boys in his class. He spent time with the boys, helped them with their homework when he could, shared with them what he was, and influenced their lives. Because of the relationships that were developed, he played a strategic role in his students' lives.

It wasn't fantastic teaching methods, and it wasn't the teacher's profound insights. But it was his genuine love, expressed through significant contacts. Dr. Hendricks attributes much of the credit for his ministry today to the impact of the relationship with that Sunday School teacher.

What does it take to be an effective Sunday School teacher? It takes a knowledge of the Bible. For without that there is no true Christian education. But in order to deeply influence students, to help them become true disciples of Jesus Christ, a teacher must cultivate deeply personal relationships with his students. What a teacher *is* matters more than what he *knows.*

The relationship of a teacher with his students is portrayed in an account written by Michael J. Boyd, and published in *The United Methodist Reporter,* April 27, 1979.

He stood before me in the small classroom of the Franklin Street Evangelical United Brethren Church—now called the United Methodist Church—of Union City, Ohio. One by one, he called upon each boy assembled to read Bible verses and lesson elements. On my part, it was more of an act of courtesy than a sincere attempt to find a true meaning for Christian living that I read for him.

Yet, Harry Porter, my Sunday School teacher, exemplifies that true Christian person that we all should strive to be. In many ways, it was not what he said in those Sunday School classes that impressed me, but his overall Christian manhood that helped guide me toward our heavenly Father. For all this strong Christian example, I thank God every day.

In the first place, I now realize that Harry is an honest person. In fact, his gentle, truthful manner frequently transcended from church to Wednesday evening baseball, which he organized for the boys of the church.

For example, if Umpire Porter called us out on strikes, we frequently argued. But his sincere nature usually calmed us with this reply: "That's the way I saw it!" Through many church activities, which he planned and organized himself, Harry maintained a warm, honest relationship with us.

Moreover, I now realize just how dedicated Harry is to the church and our loving Father. Recently, he told me that he wanted to be a school teacher, but the Great Depression altered his plans. Since I believe that Christ calls many teachers into His service, I am convinced that He called Harry to serve Him as a Sunday School teacher. I truly felt the dedicated concern that Harry must have felt for me long ago when he shared with me some of his trials and tribulations of teaching young people today.

Most of all, I admire Harry's quiet humility. Although his quiet manner could be misconstrued for shyness, I now realize that it is because of a close, humble relationship that he shares with our heavenly Father that extends itself toward those around him. In short, Harry Porter is a man with a sincere mind, dedicated heart, and humble spirit.

I shall always remember my Sunday School teacher! (7, no. 20, p. 2)

12
Sunday School and Lay Leadership

We can learn many things from history or we may elect to ignore the lessons that it teaches. If we ignore these lessons, we are cut off from the benefit of our predecessors' experiences. But if we review these experiences, we can benefit from observing the consequences of actions. For we can evaluate consequences best when we have the perspective of time and distance.

History teaches us several things about the Sunday School. It teaches us the importance of a strong emphasis on Bible content in the Sunday School. And it teaches us the value of building relationships within the context of the church. When Bible instruction and meaningful relationships are united, there is the potential for a ministry that has a powerful and dramatic impact in a person's life.

The third lesson we need to understand is the essential role that lay persons play in this ministry. When Clarence Benson listed the three characteristics that distinguished the Sunday School movement from all other religious movements, he cited the reliance upon lay leadership as the first characteristic. Without lay leadership there would have been no Sunday School *(Popular History,* p. 119).

The Shoe Salesman

Dwight L. Moody is an example of the strategic nature of lay involvement. Moody influenced the course of American church history as few men have done. Through the continuing results of his evangelistic campaigns and a variety of organizations that he helped to establish, he continues to influence our nation today. A product of a Sunday School teacher's concern, he went on to be a dominant influence in the Sunday School movement.

As a not-too-promising shoe salesman, Moody was challenged by the statement, "The world has yet to see what God can do with just one man who would give himself completely in His service." And Mr. Moody determined by the grace of God to be that man.

At first he found it difficult to express that commitment through the Sunday School. When he asked his pastor about the possibility of teaching Sunday School, Moody was told that there were no Sunday School classes available. The pastor told him to wait and that perhaps one would become available. Moody replied that he would build a class from unchurched children, if he were only given a room. He was granted permission to use the boiler room in the church.

And he did just what he said he would. He built the class so that it soon outgrew the boiler room. When he asked for more space, he was told there was none available. So he found a saloon that was not being used on Sunday mornings. Perhaps for his students, the intrigue of attending Sunday School class in a saloon contributed to the success of Moody's class, for they soon outgrew that "classroom."

From the saloon Moody moved to an empty store. By now he had built the class to the size of a school and he needed assistance. So he secured helpers and expanded his ministry. Before long Mr. Moody built the class that had begun in a boiler room into one of the largest Sunday Schools in America. A layman had reached Moody, and, as a layman, Moody personally demonstrated the potential in lay leadership for the Sunday School.

Lay People Are the Lifeblood

And there are Moodys today. They are in our churches looking and waiting for the challenge to make an impact upon the world. The strategic nature of lay persons in the ministry has not changed through the years. They are still the lifeblood of the Sunday School. James Murch wrote, "The latent capacities of Christian laymen and laywomen in thousands of churches constitute an unmined lode of treasure" *(Teach or Perish,* p. 74). And Sunday School ministry can still challenge these lay persons.

It is the lay instructor who can provide the balance in a church ministry. Most churches have one, or at the most two, paid staff members. If they do all of the instruction, the church will suffer from a limited perspective. And those paid staff members will soon collapse from exhaustion. But as lay men and women become involved, they broaden the perspective on instruction. They communicate with those whom the paid staff members never reach. And they spread the work load so that more gets done and responsibilities are distributed among many persons.

This is not to imply that teaching is the only ministry in the church. There are many different ministries and all are important. And none is more important than the preaching of the Word. Near the end of the last century, H. Clay Trumbull stressed the important place of both teaching and preaching in the history of the church from the time of Christ on.

Trumbull wrote, "Christians have been aroused from their sloth, and sinners have been startled in and from their sins, by the clarion voice of the herald-preacher. Preaching has been, and is, and is to be, the preeminent agency for the warning and calling of sinners, and for the exhorting and directing of saints. But the religious *training* of any people has been attained, and the results of any great reformation have been made permanent, only through a process of interlocutory, or catechetical, *teaching;* such as forms the distinguishing characteristics of the technical Sunday School" *(Yale Lectures,* p. 67). What Trumbull wrote almost 100 years ago is true today. And it is lay teachers who will do this teaching.

Building the Church

But probably the most important reason for recruiting lay teachers is to fulfill the biblical principles for the building of the church. In his letter to the Ephesians, Paul wrote that Christ gives leadership gifts to certain persons in the body of Christ. These individuals have special abilities to help prepare other Christians to fulfill their responsibilities. Christ gives these leadership gifts "for the equipping of the saints for the work of service, to the building up of the body of Christ" (Eph. 4:12). And it is only as believers are prepared to serve, and then are serving, that any individual church will fulfill its mission and accomplish its potential.

The involvement of lay persons in ministry is not optional. It is a COMMAND! And the church that ignores the command is ignoring the most basic guideline for the administration of a church. Lay leaders must comprise the heart of any ministry within the church. And the clear lesson of history is that they are the secret of success for the Sunday School, a vital program of the church.

Teacher Preparation

In order for the Sunday School program to fulfill its potential, there has to be a core of teachers prepared to serve. The quality of their ministry will depend upon the depth of their commitment. These teachers need to be deeply committed so that they can achieve their greatest potential and so that their church can thrive.

1. Bible knowledge. But teachers will be frustrated unless they are equipped with the necessary tools to succeed. The first of these is biblical knowledge. A teacher doesn't need to be a biblical scholar, but he does need to know the basic principles of the Word. Beyond that, a willingness to study the Word in preparation for teaching is absolutely imperative. And this doesn't mean 15 minutes a week glancing over the teacher's manual.

A teacher who is going to teach out of adequate knowledge needs to commit himself to spending as much time each week as necessary. In order to facilitate this study, some basic books are needed. Every teacher should own his own copy of a reliable contemporary translation of the Bible, such as the *New American Standard Bible.* He should also own an exhaustive concordance, a topical concordance, a Bible dictionary, a Bible handbook, and a Bible atlas. And when he knows what he will teach, he must then plan effective methods to teach it well.

2. Relationship-building. In addition to Bible knowledge, a teacher must commit himself to spending enough time to build significant relationships with the students. While it takes time to do this, the rewards are significant and long lasting. The rewards are the students' lives that will be transformed. There is no way that the professional staff members of a church can ever hope to get to know all church members in depth. And yet a teacher of a class can get to know each student in that class. The ministry of the Sunday School and the entire church will become stronger because of these relationships. The Christian teacher will be faithful to his responsibility to minister, and the student will grow through the discipling process.

The Mission—Christian Education

In order to experience the depth of ministry that can result from significant lay involvement, each Christian must come to understand what Christian education is and how it is an integral part of the mission of the Church.

Dr. Roy Zuck, in *The Holy Spirit in Your Teaching,* has given a definition of Christian education that applies well to the Sunday School. He defined evangelical Christian education as, "the Christ-centered, Bible-based, pupil-related process of communicating God's written Word through the power of the Holy Spirit, for the purpose of leading pupils to Christ, and building them up in Christ" (Scripture Press, 1963, p. xi).

It is important that laymen recognize that Christian education is the mission of the Church. Because only then will a new dimension of enthusiasm and purpose characterize their teaching. Christian education is not some peripheral program superimposed upon the ministry of the church. It is not optional. It is the very heart of ministry, because it means leading students to Christ and then helping them grow toward spiritual maturity. Only as laymen are involved in this manner will our Sunday Schools and churches succeed in accomplishing their mission.

The involvement of all lay persons in a given church will produce the results described in Ephesians 4:15-16: "But speaking the truth in love, we are to grow up in all aspects into Him, who is the head, even Christ, from whom the whole body, being fitted and held together by that which every joint supplies, according to the proper working of each individual part, causes the growth of the body for the building up of itself in love."

Pros and Cons

The Sunday School has been the most powerful educational agency of the local church for nearly 200 years. The vast majority of churches presently conduct Sunday Schools and countless students are coming to know Christ and growing spiritually through them. The Sunday School ministry is at the heart of the mission of the Church, and it mobilizes lay people in a way that no other ministry ever has been able to do.

And yet Sunday School has its detractors. There are pessimists who foretell its imminent demise. However, Sunday School has much in common with Mark Twain who related to a friend that the reports of his death had been greatly exaggerated. We could describe Sunday School in the words of another great American, Pogo, who said, "We have met the enemy, and it is us." If Sunday School is weak, perhaps it is because we fail to make it work. Clarence Benson has stated that the Sunday School has worked. And it has worked both inside and outside the church. And it can work today.

Nothing Succeeds like Success

We need committed workers today who have the vision of men like Robert Raikes. He saw a need and developed a program to meet that need. And then he worked very hard at making his suggestions work. Only after demonstrated success did he talk about his ideas. But some persons today suggest eliminating the Sunday School and propose either no alternatives or superficial ones at best. We must do more than talk. We must work. And we must concentrate our efforts in areas where we can see some hope of success.

As committed evangelicals we must speak to the problems that people face today. And we must speak clearly. Around us we see hopelessness and despair. Divorce, suicide, frustration, and anxiety are commonplace. But God has answers for these and other problems. Sunday School has been a powerful ministry in the past to speak to people's needs and this ministry continues today. But the voice of Sunday School is valuable only as it speaks the message of the Bible. When the truth of God's Word is applied to the real issues of life, then people can confront and successfully deal with their problems.

The Church Spoke

When godlessness and despair characterized the first century, the New Testament church spoke. And as it spoke clearly, that society was transformed by the evangelistic and teaching ministries of the New Testament church. The first century Christians were described by unbelievers as those who "have turned the world upside down" (Acts 17:6, KJV).

In the 16th century when society and the life of the institutional church were corrupt, Luther and other reformers spoke with a biblical voice, and made an impact that continues today upon the world. They spoke and did not stutter. And as their message was received and applied, society and the world were changed. Their call was a challenge to obey the Bible. They proposed evangelism and Bible teaching. And they ministered effectively.

In the 18th century when life in England was bleak, John Wesley, Robert Raikes, and others saw the need. They conducted a ministry of evangelism and education. And Christians, obeying God's Word, again turned the world upside down. When there were great problems to be solved, the solution included applying the truth of God's Word. And the solution included laymen.

In the 19th century the United States was expanding its borders. Hundreds of thousands of families were left with no source of religious instruction, or any other instruction either. And the Sunday School movement, spread by missionaries like Stephen Paxson and a hundred others, established Sunday Schools to evangelize and teach those families. Thus, the ministry of Sunday School influenced the course of a nation.

Light and Darkness

Christians, through a ministry of evangelism and instruction in the Word, have established beachheads against sin, immorality, and ignorance. It is easy for us to forget, in the sophistication of the 20th century, that there still is a conflict between light and darkness. The forces of evil continue unabated in the world, and they will increase. But as the world grows darker, the light of the Gospel will shine more brightly.

And it is the responsibility of every Christian to participate in shining forth the light of the Word of God. The ministry of Sunday School continues as an effective and powerful beacon shining light into the nooks and crannies of humanity.

The truth of God's Word and its ability to meet people's needs is something to get excited about. Because the Word of God is powerful and effective, it must be communicated. But we have no idea how much longer we have to share the Word. We have no way of knowing how long the current openness to Bible teaching will continue. And we have no way of knowing when Christ will return.

Christians would be wise to take advantage of the Sunday School structure and get on with the business of making it work. We must teach the Bible to those who need to know. Teachers must build relationships so that the truth of the Bible can be demonstrated through their lives. And churches must mobilize a vast force of lay persons, persons who are willing to take the mission of the church seriously and make disciples through evangelism and teaching the Word.

Just because there are flaws in the system doesn't mean that we should scrap it. Any system devised and implemented by humans will be imperfect. Sunday School has its weaknesses, but Christians know of its effectiveness, and it is functioning in most churches. The principles upon which Sunday School is built pervade both the Old and New Testaments, and the history of the Church. We must work diligently at improving Sunday Schools and helping them become as effective as possible. We must teach the Word, and we must do it to the glory of God.

This means planning programs that will effectively accomplish the mission of the church through Christian education. Larry Richards has emphasized that teaching biblical concepts requires personal example. *"This is why Christian education is an interpersonal ministry.* This is why when we design Christian education systems, we *must* provide for exploration of the Word in a relational context, in which the liveable reality of God's words can be seen and experienced through others" *(A Theology of Christian Education,* Zondervan, 1975, p. 45).

In order to accomplish this, we must help every person to discover and develop his spiritual gift of ministry to build up the body of Christ. Ray C. Stedman described a goal of the Sunday School at

Peninsula Bible Church in Palo Alto, California. "Our entire Sunday School is set up to equip the saints of all ages, to do the work of the ministry" *(Body Life,* Regal Books, 1972, p. 86). He described how this church was begun with the deep conviction from Ephesians 4 that the work of the ministry belonged to the people not the pastor *(Ibid.,* p. 133).

And even beyond these philosophical considerations, we must work at improving the mechanics of Sunday School ministries. We must prepare our teachers well. We must take advantage of all appropriate methodology and techniques that are available to us in our electronic age. We must seek to involve families and strengthen Christian education in the home. We must use high quality curriculum materials to help us teach the Bible and build relationships as effectively as possible. We must evaluate the administrative structures—the time that Sunday Schools meet, the places that they meet—and we must be willing to make appropriate changes. In short, we must do everything that we can to improve the quality of Sunday Schools.

The report of a panel interview with Dr. Carl Henry was published in *Christianity Today* on August 18, 1967. He said, "The Sunday School offers hope and light, and its light needs to be turned up so Jesus Christ and the Bible are kept at the center of human need." He continued, "Much about our age is drab and dismal, but the Sunday School, for all its faults, remains the one hopeful beacon in the darkness of these times" (p. 11).

James Murch recognized that, "The early church accepted its educational task and discharged its obligation with complete dedication motivated by the conviction that Christ was coming soon. It was spurred by the imperative that men must be taught and saved ere it was too late to teach and save at all. It was a case of *teach* or *perish*" *(Teach or Perish,* p. 65).

The mandate continues. We do not have an option. God has commanded His church to teach His Word. And we must do it with haste—with a sense of conviction and urgency. For there is no other answer to the deepest questions confronting humanity. God has chosen to work through fallible humans using imperfect programs. But as we teach God's Word through these programs, God blesses our efforts and the results. The Sunday School is an effective tool and can

268.09
W735

66224

c. 1

be used to accomplish God's will. The Sunday School is 200 years old—and still counting. Still counting birthdays, and still counting for God.